W9-BQZ-609

Reading Laboratory

P.205

READING PROBLEMS

AND

PROBLEM READERS

by

M. F. W. POLLACK, M.A.
The Readwell System, San Mateo, California

and

JOSEPHINE A. PIEKARZ, Ph.D.
New York University, New York, New York

DAVID McKAY COMPANY, INC.

New York

READING PROBLEMS AND PROBLEM READERS

LIBRARY OF CONGRESS CATALOG CARD NUMBER: 63-15599

MANUFACTURED IN THE UNITED STATES OF AMERICA

VAN REES PRESS   •   NEW YORK

To the memory of my father,

EDGAR A. POLLACK

for whom reading,
and thinking about
what he read, was
a way of life.

Preface

THIS BOOK was written because the authors firmly believe that most retarded readers can be helped to overcome their reading difficulties. It is all about reading problems and problem readers. It has been written especially for the parents and classroom teachers of problem readers, so that they can better understand what can be done to help these children. Parents and teachers are frequently perplexed, frustrated, and discouraged by reading problems. Because parents may not be aware of what can be done for retarded readers and where to seek help, many children may not have an opportunity to overcome their reading problems and may be doomed to permanent illiteracy. It is hoped that this book will make it possible for a larger number of poor readers to receive help, so that they may become independent and contributing members of our society.

Skill in reading is a necessity in our society. Written material continually surrounds us, and a person who cannot read is seriously handicapped. A severe reading deficiency affects the personal adjustment and accomplishments of a person to a far greater extent than do many other handicaps. The large numbers of deficient readers among school drop-outs, juvenile delinquents, prison inmates, and people on welfare are evidence of this. In fact, one of the most pressing social problems of our literate and technological civilization is finding employment for people who cannot read or who have only limited reading ability. This book was written to explain why people become reading problems and what can be done to help them.

This is not a how-to-do-it book. It is not designed to give specific directions for the diagnosing and correcting of reading problems; rather, its aim is to develop insights and understandings, so that both parents and classroom teachers will be better prepared to understand their problem readers and the difficulties that besiege them. Increased understanding, hopefully, will lead to an intelligent solution of problems and will aid in decreasing parental and teacher frustration and anxiety.

It is impossible to understand and appreciate the difficulties encountered by a retarded reader without knowing something about the complexities involved in reading our language and the many reasons that contribute to reading failure. For this reason, this book is divided into three major parts. The introductory part discusses the nature of reading and the causes of reading retardation. It emphasizes the fact that reading problems are caused by a multitude of interacting factors and that each retarded reader has his unique combination of problems.

The second part of this book consists of a series of illustrative case histories. They were selected to demonstrate different kinds of reading problems and different kinds of problem readers. The case studies are presented simply and honestly with a minimum of technical terminology, clinical clichés, or psychological jargon. The reports describe the problems the pupils experienced and what was done for them at the reading clinic where they received help.

The third part suggests specific means for combating the problem of poor reading by setting up reading laboratories.

The authors wish to thank the pupils whose case histories are included here. Without them, this book would not have been possible. May it please them to know that because of their reading difficulties, other children will be helped to overcome their problems. We also wish to thank those teachers and consultants who, as members of the staff of the Readwell Clinic, contributed so much to the development of *The Readwell System*. In particular, grateful recognition is due Mrs. Edgar Pollack, Constance Price, Ann Simmons, George Mc-Murry, and Edna Carroll.

Contents

PART I

Introduction

1

The Nature of Reading

TEACHING people how to read English is not easy. Even adults who are already fluent in reading another language often find written English arbitrary and baffling. And American children, when first faced with the necessity of associating the spoken with the written language, also find the task confusing and difficult. As a result, the teaching of reading has been a controversial issue in the United States ever since compulsory education became effective. Since that time, our schools have been expected to teach all of the children of all of the people how to read. This is a large undertaking.

Before the days of compulsory school attendance, children who experienced difficulty in learning to read simply dropped out of school. They lived out their lives as illiterates or, at best, semiliterates. The children who remained in school learned to read by whatever methods their teachers employed or by figuring out the reading process by themselves, often in spite of the teaching methods. In fact, in those days, teachers "listened to children's lessons." This implies that children were expected to learn on their own; the teacher's primary function was to see that they did. If pupils weren't learning, they were sent back to their seats for additional self-help. By rote memorizing and by struggling to grasp the relationship between speech and print, those children who survived in school learned to read.

Compulsory school attendance, however, meant that children were required to remain in school whether they were successful students or not. Now teachers had to do more than listen to lessons; they had to bestir themselves to teach those children who could not teach themselves. When taught, some of these children learned easily; however, others still experienced difficulty. Various methods were tried and controversies arose concerning the "best" way to teach reading to all children. Arguments often became heated as people championed a rigid phonic approach, the look-and-say method, or a sentence and story approach. The less that people knew about the reading process itself, the more loudly they argued in favor of their pet method. Although some controversy still exists today, and critics of education are still plentiful, most of the criticism comes from people who are uninformed about reading and the way it is taught by most teachers in most schools.

Development of Writing

To understand the complexities involved in learning to read English, it is necessary to understand the development of language and the relationship between spoken and written languages. Language as we know it is one of the major factors that distinguishes man from all other creatures. The language faculty became possible only with the most recent evolutionary additions to man's neurological system. Languages are man-invented and must be learned by each individual in much the

4

same order as language itself evolved. In the beginning, people communicated with each other through gestures and random sounds in the same way that lower forms of life do. Gradually, the need developed for more systematic and precise communication, and people responded to the need by putting sounds together in ordered sequences to represent things and ideas. In this way, spoken language developed. Words are therefore tags or labels for things and ideas, and spoken words consist of arbitrary combinations of sounds. As people developed new things and ideas, they made up words to represent them by combining sounds in new sequences; thus, they continued to add to their language.

Eventually, people felt a need to record language in order to communicate with people at a distance without the necessity of actually visiting them. They also wanted to preserve their ideas and accomplishments for future generations. In the absence of tape recorders, phonographs, and other technological equipment, they were forced to develop a system for recording speech with the tools at hand, and visual symbols were invented. In fact, if mechanical means of recording sound had been available, it is highly probable that writing would never have developed. There would have been no need for it.

The first attempts at written communication were pictures. Things and ideas were represented directly through drawings. People who recognized the pictured objects and their relationships to each other could communicate with each other, even though they could not speak or understand each other's spoken languages or dialects. However, picture writing had many limitations and shortcomings. At best, it was vague and inexact. Abstractions and subtleties were difficult to depict. Only simple, concrete ideas could be effectively communicated. There was a need for a more accurate way of recording things and ideas in visual form. Speech itself had to be recorded in some

5

way, since speech was a more precise form of communication.

The course of history saw several different systems used for the visual recording of speech; the major ones were word-concept writing and alphabetic writing. Word-concept writing used ideographs, an early form of the hieroglyph. Ideographs were graphic symbols which represented things and ideas directly rather than the spoken words for these things and ideas. The ancient, classical Chinese logographs were examples of ideographs, as are our numeral figures and other arbitrary symbols. For instance, *3* stands for the concept of three and not for the spoken word. In Germany it is called *drei,* in France it is called *trois;* in other languages it may be called *tres* or *kolme.* The written figures *2, 3, 4,* etc. are universally understood, because they represent concepts rather than spoken words. Written languages based on ideographs have as many ideographs as there are words in the language; a separate ideograph represents each word of the language. The ideographs are arranged arbitrarily and in a variety of directions: from left to right, right to left, or up and down. Reading languages recorded in this way involves recalling the concepts represented by each ideograph. Since most languages include thousands of words, learning to read these languages involves rote memorization of thousands of characters, many of which, to the uninitiated, seem similar in appearance. If forgotten by a reader, the characters need to be rememorized, since there is no logical relationship between the appearance of the written symbol and the concept it represents. Learning to read such languages is a gargantuan task, and literacy is the exception rather than the rule in countries utilizing this form of writing.

In contrast to word writing, alphabetic writing is based on the concept that speech or spoken language consists of sounds that are put together in different sequences and combinations to constitute the spoken words of a language. Each word con-

6

sists of a fixed combination of sounds. The basic sounds of any language are not numerous. The same few sounds are put together in different combinations to pronounce all the words of a language. Of the 2800 different languages that are spoken throughout the world, the majority is comprised of between fifteen and fifty different sounds, although the number of words in any language may total over one hundred thousand, depending upon the level of the culture. Since words represent things and ideas, and sophisticated cultures possess a greater number of things and ideas, advanced civilizations have the largest number of words in their languages. Primitive cultures have few things and ideas and, as a result, have limited vocabularies. The same holds true on an individual basis. The brighter or more sophisticated a person is, the more he tends to know; the more he knows, the larger his vocabulary.

In alphabetic writing, letter symbols represent the sounds, or phonemes, of the spoken language. The letters, or alphabetic characters, are recorded in the same sequence as the sounds of the spoken words, and spaces are left between groups of letters to separate one word from another. Alphabetic writing is manually and visually recorded speech. Reading alphabetic writing involves making the correct associations between the letter symbols and the sounds they represent. In a perfectly consistent phonetic system, there are as many different letters in the written language as there are sounds in the spoken language; each letter represents a specific sound and each sound is always represented by the same letter. Modern Italian and Turkish each use twenty-seven letters for the twenty-seven basic sounds of their languages. Modern Spanish, Bohemian, and Finnish are also highly consistent and regular. Others have less consistency and regularity. German uses thirty-eight different symbols for the thirty-six basic sounds of its language and Russian (since 1918) uses thirty-six symbols for its thirty-four

7

basic sounds. Still other languages such as modern Greek, French, and English have extremely irregular and arbitrary systems. American English uses twenty-six different letters to represent the forty-five sounds of its spoken language. The forty-five sounds are spelled in approximately 350 different ways. The sound of long *a* (ā), for example, is spelled differently in each of the following words: *a, aye, eh,* m*ai*d, th*ey,* n*eigh,* f*e*te, pl*ay*. There are thirty or thirty-five different spellings for this sound. On the other hand, the letter *a* represents other sounds and serves different functions in these words: *hat, said, along, are*. This confusion is further compounded when the appearance of each letter may change from lower case to upper case, from cursive writing to manuscript writing, from Bodoni print to Monarch. This does not mean, however, that the English language is not alphabetic or phonetic. It merely means that there is not a one-to-one relationship between letter and sound and that it therefore takes longer and is more difficult to learn the correct associations between what is seen and what is heard in the English language than in many other languages. The letters, however arbitrarily they seem to be put together, still represent sounds; so our language is phonetic. Learning to read English involves not only becoming acquainted with the letters of the written language and the sounds of the spoken language but also learning the various circumstances and conditions under which particular letters and combinations of letters represent particular sounds. Such knowledge is gained through a study of what is usually called phonics and structural analysis. In addition, however, it is possible to identify printed words with the aid of configuration clues, picture clues, meaning clues, or through phonetic respelling in dictionaries. There are no other ways of recognizing printed words independently. The only alternative open to the reader who cannot identify words through one or another of these means is to ask someone to tell

8

him the unknown words. Good readers do not rely exclusively on any one of these means—not even phonics—but use all available means in combination for rapid and efficient word identification.

Reading Controversies

The various controversies concerning the teaching of reading center around *which one of the above-listed means* should be taught as the sole approach for identifying printed words. The "Look-and-Say" or "Whole-Word" advocates wish to emphasize the use of configuration clues to the exclusion of all other word-identification techniques. The "Sentence" or "Story" protagonists lean heavily on meaning or contextual clues. The "Phonetic Fanatics" think that success in reading is possible only through a rigid and concentrated phonetic approach. The fact is, however, that our written language does not lend itself to the exclusive application of any one of these techniques, and all techniques must be taught to all children if they are to become good readers.

Beyond the first few words, configuration clues alone soon cease to be useful, because too many words look alike in our written language. With only twenty-six letters to spell all the words of the language, similarities in the appearance of words cannot be avoided. Picture and meaning clues cannot be used in isolation, since many words in our language have similar meanings and the same concept may frequently be expressed by several different words. On the other hand, no amount of phonetic or structural knowledge will enable a reader to identify words like *tear* and *rebel* correctly unless he has knowledge of the context. Each of these techniques works best when used in conjunction with other techniques of word recognition.

The Reading Process

The reading process, however, consists of more than the identification of printed words. It is a complex process, the composite of many interrelated subskills that might be classified under the headings of word recognition, understanding, fluency, and study skills. Unless meaning is derived, it cannot be said that reading has taken place. Therefore, as letter symbols are associated with speech sounds, so must the meaning of the spoken words be associated with the written symbols. People have argued that efficient adult readers get ideas or meaning directly from printed words and that sounds play no part in the process of reading. This is a complete misunderstanding of the nature of our written language. The letter symbols represent sounds, not meanings. Pictures represent things and ideas directly. The characters in classical Chinese represent meanings or concepts, but the letters in English writing represent meaningless sounds. The way to get at the meaning is to pronounce the sounds represented by the letter symbols. A person who cannot do this cannot get meaning from printed words.

When a person has practiced making associations between symbols and sounds successfully for a long time, he does it so quickly, easily, efficiently, and automatically that when reading silently, he is no longer consciously aware of individual letters and sounds, and he feels that he is gaining meaning directly from the printed forms of words and phrases. A beginning reader cannot do this, since a child lacks the necessary years of practice. He must make the associations between letters and sounds consciously, often with great deliberation and effort. In fact, he often becomes so preoccupied by this task, because of the many inconsistencies in our written language, that he fails to grasp any meaning at all. Once he can make the necessary symbol-sound associations readily, he will be able to follow the meaning. The more readily he can make the associations, the less aware will he be of doing so, until he becomes so proficient that he, too, will think that he gets meaning directly from printed words, phrases, or sentences as he reads silently.

Incidentally, silent reading is a relatively recent phenomenon in language development, probably representing the most advanced stage of language. It was not until the Middle Ages that people learned to read without reading aloud. In recapitulating the linguistic development of the species, a child learns to read aloud before he learns to read silently. A child first listens and then responds to oral language. Gradually he learns to speak, but only after he has progressed through a stage of random babbling sounds. Then he learns to read aloud and to write. Only then is he ready for the most highly developed language skill—silent reading. Omission of any of these stages of development frequently leads to language problems. Non-oral approaches to the initial teaching of reading ignore and deny the nature of our written language and the sequence of language development, as do pressures for too early silent reading.

While the identification of printed words is a fairly mechanical procedure and, barring gross deficiencies, can be taught to almost everyone, understanding the meanings conveyed by the words depends upon many factors. For one thing, understanding involves a literal comprehension or grasp of explicitly stated facts. It also involves interpretation. Interpretation refers to meanings that are implied by the writer and must be inferred by the reader. In addition, understanding includes critical evaluation based on some sort of external criteria. Understanding, or comprehending, goes beyond being able to retell a story accurately or being able to report clearly-stated facts. By teaching people to read, we multiply tremendously the number of external influences that reach their minds. We are therefore obligated to teach them how to interpret, judge, and evaluate the

11

ideas they encounter. To be able to do this requires a certain amount of reasoning ability and a fund of background information and knowledge. If a person cannot see relationships and make associations between things, ideas, and events from his own experience and those on the page in front of him, he cannot grasp implied meanings. Nor will he be able to evaluate what he reads if he has not accumulated sufficient knowledge to make judgments. Interpretation and critical thinking cannot be carried on in the absence of background knowledge.

Individual intellectual and experiential capacities place limitations on how much meaning people will derive from what they read. Some people will be able to derive only literal, surface meanings; others will be able to grasp many inferential and connotative meanings. These limitations, however, are not inherent in the written language or even unique to reading. They are related to the thinking processes. There are no meanings or understandings in written material that do not at the same time exist first in spoken language. If a person understands what he hears, he will grasp the same concept when he reads.

Closely related to meaning are all the study skills, which are essentially the utilization of reading for learning purposes. These are the skills which ultimately distinguish successful students from less successful ones. They include the skills involved in the location of information; the selection, interpretation, and evaluation of information; the organization of information; and the retention of information. Students must know how to work efficiently with reading materials in the various subject areas, particularly in science, mathematics, social studies, and literature. The reading of simple, narrative selections will not necessarily enable them to do this. The high-school or college student who cannot find required information in available textbooks by utilizing library resources and textbook aids, who cannot evaluate information for relevancy, who cannot distinguish major ideas from minor details, and who cannot arrange his information in a form which points up the difference between the significant and the less significant, is very likely to be a weak student and one who spends unnecessary amounts of time in studying. Gaining study skills cannot be left to chance. They must be taught specifically and directly as a part of the reading and learning process.

If reading is to be an enjoyable activity and pursued voluntarily, it must be performed easily and efficiently. Good readers are seldom slow, laborious readers; slow, laborious readers seldom enjoy reading. Fluency in reading is the culmination of proficiency in word recognition, understanding, and certain study skills and involves more than speed. It makes no more sense to read everything too rapidly than to read everything too slowly. The efficient reader can and does read rapidly when he needs to and slowly when he needs to, shifting his speed according to the kind and difficulty of material and his purpose for reading it. At times he may skip and skim and read selectively; at other times he may read not only slowly and thoroughly but reread selected portions of material. Only as he is able to do this will he be able to cope with the tremendous amount of material that is published at the present time and be able to use it for his purposes.

It is the school's responsibility, therefore, to teach all of these skills as part of the reading program. Children who miss out on any of these skills for any reason whatever are handicapped academically, and many of life's opportunities are closed to them. College entrance, for example, is forbidden to students whose academic averages are low. The college diploma, symbol of success and passport to many occupations and professions, is often withheld from students who lack reading skill. Parents as well as teachers are becoming increasingly aware of the importance of reading skills for success in many areas. Greater efforts are being made to provide adequate instruction in regular classrooms. In addition, many people seek help from special reading services where highly trained personnel do remedial work, often with the aid of specialized equipment. It is gratifying to know that most children can and do learn to read well when they are provided with the necessary instruction.

2

Causes of Reading Problems

Iᴛ has been estimated that about one-third of all elementary-school students in the United States are retarded readers. At the high-school level there are also large numbers of pupils who read inadequately, although the proportion at this level is not as high as at the elementary-school level, since many pupils drop out of school as a result of their reading problems. /Retarded readers are pupils who, for various reasons, have failed to acquire the necessary reading skill, and who, therefore, underachieve not only in reading but in all subject areas that are dependent upon reading. Many of these children are not only average in intelligence but may be even above average. They come from homes at all socio-economic levels and attend both large and small schools. The one thing they share in common is that they read at a level well below their expected potential.

Research into the causes of reading problems has been carried on intensively for the past twenty-five years. The findings of research indicate that there are many reasons why children fail to learn to read at a level consistent with their capabilities. Any factor or condition that can interfere with any kind of learning is apt to have even more influence on the acquisition of reading skills than on other learning. Since reading is a highly complex process which involves the use of abstract symbols and requires highly disciplined eye movements and close, concentrated attention for prolonged periods of time, the effects of negative factors and conditions are exaggerated. Furthermore, the causes of reading difficulties may differ from one pupil to another, not only within the same classroom but even among siblings. These causes may be physical, psychological, intellectual, or environmental in nature. They may be factors inherent in the child himself or they may be external factors related to conditions at home, in the community, or at school.

The multiple-causation theory of reading retardation is generally accepted. This theory states that usually several negative factors operate jointly to prevent a child from learning how to read. If a child has a single handicap, he may compensate for it in some way and thus learn despite his difficulty. When several handicapping factors exist simultaneously, however, they form an insurmountable obstacle, and the child cannot overcome them and learn successfully. Therefore, it is not at all uncommon in diagnosing reading problems to discover that a child is struggling under several handicaps, most of which have to be eliminated before he can be taught to read. The greater the number and severity of causal factors, the more serious the reading problem tends to be and the more difficult it is to overcome. In addition, adverse factors act selectively on children who possess certain other negative factors. For example, poor vision may interfere with the reading development of some children more than with others, depending upon what related problems they have.

Another generalization that has emerged from research findings is that although handicapping factors may be identified

16

within a child, they may bear little relation to his reading problem. The correction or elimination of such factors may still leave a child unable to learn to read. The pattern of factors involved seems to be more important than any single factor or condition for such children. Fortunately, however, the greater number of retarded readers manage successfully to overcome their reading problems when conditions are favorable and when suitable instruction is provided.

The causes frequently found to be responsible in part or in whole for reading problems may be classified in several different ways. A simple classification might include the following areas: physical, psychological, intellectual, and environmental. Many different specific factors and conditions worthy of mention are subsumed under each of these headings.

Physical Factors

Since reading is dependent upon the successful identification of visual symbols, good vision is very important. Our eyes, however, were originally designed to be used mainly for looking at things at various distances, and when they were employed for close viewing, it was primarily for point work. Our eyes were not expected to move any more than was necessary to see what our fingers were doing. The process of reading, however, requires that our eyes be used in a thoroughly arbitrary and unnatural manner. During our lifetime, there is probably nothing that our eyes are required to do that is more demanding and taxing than to move correctly while reading books held approximately twelve to fourteen inches from our eyes. Things viewed at a far distance do not require such highly disciplined coordination; nor do objects viewed with only one eye at near or far distances.

Each eye is an independent lens whose movements are controlled by six muscles that surround it. Single clear vision is

17

achieved when both eyes are focused correctly. As the eyes move, the twelve muscles have to realign the two eyes to permit clear, single vision. Since our written language is recorded in a left-to-right direction, reading our language requires moving our eyes from left to right in smooth forward jumps, or fixations, across the closely packed lines of print. With each fixation, the twelve muscles must continually realign the eyes. Furthermore, they must do this while the eyes are in a cramped position for prolonged periods of time. Intended originally for distance use, our eyes are relaxed when looking at objects twenty feet away. When following lines of closely packed print at a distance of only one foot, the eyes must converge considerably to see clearly. It is obvious, therefore, that vision adequate for reading purposes implies more than visual acuity or keenness of vision. Binocular coordination is also a requisite.

Research findings indicate that nearsightedness and successful academic achievement tend to be related. This may be true because nearsighted children, rather than farsighted children, are more comfortable doing near-point activities. Greater visual comfort probably encourages nearsighted youngsters to spend more time on reading activities. Nearsightedness also suggests that these children are less easily distracted by surrounding stimuli and, therefore, concentrate on their work more successfully. Research findings also indicate that very few school-age children have undetected refractive problems. Nearsightedness, farsightedness, and astigmatism are picked up readily by many of the visual screening instruments that are popularly used in schools. Moreover, all refractionists check on these conditions and make corrections when necessary. As a result, very few children in regular classrooms at the present time have problems stemming from lack of visual acuity.

It is estimated, however, that from one-third to two-thirds of all school-age children suffer from some degree of binocular incoordination severe enough to interfere with the efficient use of their eyes for reading purposes. Furthermore, in most cases these difficulties are undetected and uncorrected. The less expensive visual screening instruments do not necessarily include tests of <u>functional vision</u>. Visual specialists, unfortunately, also frequently check only for acuity and pathological conditions and neglect to investigate the functional aspects of children's vision. Children with such handicaps experience strain and discomfort in attending to the printed page and accordingly, they avoid reading activities as much as possible. Their inability to follow lines of print and to see words correctly and clearly, together with the small amounts of time they spend on reading activities, create conditions that inevitably lead to reading problems.

Still another aspect of vision, discrimination, should be mentioned. Some children have good visual acuity and can use their eyes harmoniously as a team for reading activities but have difficulty in distinguishing similarities and differences among the things they see. Since our written language uses only twenty-six different letter symbols in varying combinations to spell all the words of the language, many words, out of necessity, look alike. Only slight and subtle differences distinguish *want* from *went, eat* from *cat, horse* from *house,* and *except* from *expect.* The child who cannot recognize and remember such differences, however, is bound to experience difficulty in learning to read.

Audition, or hearing, is likewise very closely correlated with reading achievement. It is estimated that about 10 per cent of the elementary school population has hearing deficiencies significant enough to interfere with academic learning. Obviously, the child who has a hearing loss will have difficulty in hearing instructions, explanations, directions, and discussions. Learning phonics will be particularly difficult for him. His hearing loss may also prevent him from amassing a background of general information and knowledge with which to interpret and evaluate what he reads. In fact, he may even give the appearance of dullness, since he may not be aware of much that is happening around him. Particularly during their early years, children rely heavily on their hearing for learning in school as well as out of school.

Hearing losses may be of several different varieties. Some children have a generalized hearing loss: an overall reduction in their ability to hear sounds in one or both ears. Unless all sounds are amplified, they are unaware of them. Other children experience difficulty in hearing sounds at certain frequencies only, while all other sounds are distinct and clear to them. For them, therefore, spoken words may consist of combinations of recognizable sounds alternating with mumbles. Some children have permanent hearing losses due to congenital factors, such as malformation of the hearing mechanism, while many others have temporary or intermittent losses due to infection, injury, trauma, or accumulation of wax in the ears. Hearing losses frequently accompany colds and sinus infections, as well as infections of tonsils, adenoids, and mastoids. Reduced hearing during times of such infections often means that children fail to learn the things that are taught in class during such periods.

Auditory discrimination is also an important aspect of hearing. All spoken words in our language are comprised of various combinations of only about forty-five different basic sounds. Many of these sounds are very similar. In combination with each other, many of the more than a million words that they represent are also very similar in sound. It takes a very discerning ear to hear the differences between words like *moon* and *noon, shirk* and *shirt, fan* and *van, pin* and *pen,* and so forth. Lack of adequate discrimination may be caused by either a lack of appropriate training or by maturational factors. Mounting research evidence suggests that the ability to discriminate between things both seen and heard is partially subject to maturation and develops in an orderly sequence as children grow. The development of discriminatory skills may not be completed until the ages of eight years and six months to ten years for many children. This means that children may be unable to learn certain things that depend upon the possession of auditory and visual discrimination until they have reached a more mature age.

In addition to vision and hearing, many other physiological factors are related to reading success and failure. Any conditions that sap a child's vitality and deprive him of the energy necessary to staying alert can interfere with his ability to focus his attention on learning. Chronic infections of tonsils, teeth, or any other part of the anatomy may create such a handicap. Conditions of this type also make the child more susceptible to all other diseases. Ill children, being absent from school more often than well children, find their problems are compounded. And while in school, they are unable to profit from the instruction given.

Endocrine dysfunction and inadequate rest and nutrition may also interfere with school learning, as they do with adult activities. As a rule, good health is as helpful to the beginning reader as to anyone else.

Brain damage and neurological disorganization are frequently cited as causative factors in reading disability cases. Improper development of the brain or conditions of the brain caused by injury, infection, and chemical reactions of various kinds may make it difficult, if not altogether impossible, for some children to learn to read. These conditions may develop at any time before, during, or after birth and may lead to deterioration and loss of reading ability if children have already learned to read prior to this time. Many authorities suspect that larger numbers of brain-damaged children exist than have been identified and recognized to date. Their accurate identification will have to wait for the development of improved techniques of diagnosis. Relatively little is known about the brain and how it functions in learning.

Mixed-lateral dominance, a very frequently encountered symptom, which is noted when the preferred hand is not on the same side of the body as the dominant, or sighting, eye (which is usually the controlling eye in a binocular seeing situation), is likewise believed by many authorities to be a major cause of reading problems. Some people argue that mixed laterality merely implies that consistent left-to-right habits, which are necessary for success in reading, are more difficult to establish. Other people claim that mixed laterality is symptomatic of lack of cerebral dominance and even of lack of neurological organization. They further state that language development depends upon clearly established unilaterality. Case histories are offered to show that ambidextrous children and children whose preference is for the right hand and left eye, or vice versa, are more prone to difficulties, not only in reading but in speaking and writing, than those children who are consistent in their choice of hand and eye. Evidence is offered to show that when unilaterality, either right-sided or left-sided, is established, improvement in language occurs. In any event, a large proportion of severely retarded readers demonstrate laterality confusions or, as the condition is also called, mixed dominance.

Psychological Factors

The psychological factors that are related to reading retardation are numerous. Sometimes they are easily identified, but at other times, they are vague, indefinite, and illusory. These emotional elements function under the surface, frequently in various disguised forms, undermining children's opportunities for successful learning. The effectiveness of psychological problems in halting learning lies in the fact that a child who is preoccupied with fears, anxieties, and guilt feelings cannot concentrate on learning to read. Focusing attention on a printed page and following a teacher's instructions can be managed by most children when they are relaxed, comfortable, confident, and secure. When they are under too much pressure, when their security is threatened, and when they are frustrated, they cannot focus their attention upon academic learning for sustained periods of time. Though they may be physically present in the classroom, their thoughts are rarely on the lessons in front of them. The emotional strain also drains their physical energies, making them still less able to profit from instruction.

Home conditions frequently create emotional problems for children that make them prone to reading failure. Quarreling or unstable parents, broken homes requiring divided loyalty on the part of children, neglect or rejection of children by parents, indifference or hostility of parents, overprotection or domination or anxiety on the part of parents, and unhealthy rivalry among children in a family may all create situations causing personal problems for children. In some instances, such adverse conditions may spur children on to increased academic effort for compensatory reasons, but, in general, unfavorable home conditions hinder rather than help reading progress.

Conditions in school may likewise create personal problems for children. Pupil-teacher conflicts, parent-teacher conflicts, teacher pressure for achievement, unfavorable comparison of children by teachers, and failure to adapt instruction to children's needs may all be conducive to developing an unfavorable psychological climate for learning. The frustrations attendant on a failure to learn to read also become a handicap to further learning.

23

Intellectual Factors

Intelligence tends to be related to reading achievement at all academic levels. The brighter children are, the better readers they tend to be. For this reason, reading retardation must always be determined by reference to the individual child's mental capabilities regardless of his chronological age and grade placement. Other things being equal, a ten-year-old child with average intelligence can be expected to read at a fifth-grade level. However, the same expectations cannot be held for a ten-year-old child with below-average intelligence. Such a child would not be considered a retarded reader unless his reading achievement fell significantly below his limited capacity.

Below-average intelligence can and does influence reading in several ways. Children with below-average intelligence usually are not ready to begin learning to read as early as brighter children. They are frequently unable to profit from the reading instruction given in the first grade. Automatic promotion policies have pushed children on to succeeding grades regardless of the progress they have made. Second- and third-grade teachers do not necessarily reteach the first-grade reading skills needed by these slow-learning children. These children may therefore become retarded readers before they have had a chance to succeed. Once these children reach a stage of readiness for reading, their limited intelligence permits them to make only a portion of the yearly progress that average children do. Each year they fall further behind other children even when they work up to their capacities. Their rate of learning is simply slower. It takes them longer to learn each new thing. Still another effect of below-average intelligence is that children with limited learning abilities level off at maturity at a lower level than other children. In other words, they cannot

24

reach advanced levels of reading achievement despite additional instruction and training.

School Factors

Reading problems may also arise from practices and conditions surrounding children at school. Many difficulties stem from the fact that while learning is a uniquely individual affair, teaching, out of necessity, most often is group-oriented or group-directed. Although efforts are usually made to adapt instruction to individual needs in group settings, it is sometimes very difficult to do and occasionally, children are lost in the group. Since the teacher is unable to provide the special help that a particular child may need, he is unable to profit from group instruction and falls further and further behind, becoming more frustrated and discouraged with each passing day.

Sometimes a child's learning difficulties may result from the teacher's failure to adjust the methods or materials of instruction to his special needs. Since reading is a process consisting of a number of closely interrelated skills and since people learn in different ways, all children must be taught the same skills, but they must be taught them in a variety of ways. Learning to read, as learning anything else, is accomplished by the brain, which receives its information from the sense organs. Barring abnormality, all children are equipped with all senses, although the sensitivity or perceptivity of the various senses may differ with each child. Learning to read depends more upon vision and audition than on the other senses. If reading is presented to a child in such a way that it appeals to his strongest and most highly developed sense modality, he learns readily. Teachers should discover how their pupils learn most easily and capitalize on the strengths that are possessed by each student.

The materials used for instructional purposes must be appropriate if success in reading is to be realized. Materials must be interesting, must be at the right level of difficulty, and must provide opportunities for learning the various reading skills. Children cannot learn effectively from materials that are too difficult for them. On the other hand, there is no possibility for progress if materials are too easy.

Other school-connected factors that may lead to reading problems include the amount of time spent on teaching reading and the regularity and continuity of a child's school attendance. Proficiency in reading comes from plenty of practice. A child who does not spend time reading cannot expect to become a good reader. Learning any complicated skill, whether it be playing the piano, playing tennis, or dancing, requires a great deal of practice, both independently and with teacher supervision and guidance. Furthermore, instruction must be continuous and sequential. A child who does not attend school regularly because of illness or other reasons, or who attends a succession of different schools because his family moves from place to place, may lose the continuity as well as the sequence of his instruction, and experience difficulty in learning to read.

Crowded classrooms and promotion policies may contribute to some children's reading problems. Teachers cannot give individual attention when their classroom enrollments are too high. The larger the class, the more regimented the teaching must become and the fewer the teacher's opportunities for providing individual help. Automatic promotion policies frequently mean that children get pushed to more advanced grades before they are able to do the work. If teachers do not make deliberate efforts to provide suitable materials and instruction, these children derive very little benefit from sitting through their classes.

Pupil-teacher rapport is another factor that may influence a child's reading progress. Most people learn most easily and quickly when they are taught by a teacher with whom they feel comfortable and by whom they feel accepted and liked; in a word, with whom they can identify. Occasionally, a clash of personalities occurs between a teacher and a pupil, making it difficult for them to work together. The reasons for such incompatibility are numerous and complicated. Sometimes very little can be done to relieve the situation short of separating the two.

A final factor related to the school setting is the question of the competence of teachers to teach reading. Children cannot be expected to learn to read efficiently and well unless they are given appropriate instruction. Some children can learn by themselves; some children always have. But the majority of children require specific instruction. Too often teachers are unprepared to give the instruction required. Very often the teaching of reading consists of little more than distributing books to children and identifying words for them. Such practice may increase children's sight vocabularies in a random fashion, but it certainly does not equip children to identify printed words independently nor to carry on all the other skills involved in the reading process. But teachers cannot teach what they themselves do not know and what they have never been trained to do. Teacher-training institutions frequently fail to prepare teachers for the teaching of reading by neglecting to acquaint them with all the skills of reading. As a result, when children do not make expected progress in reading, too many teachers are unable to do more than distribute books, tell words, and look on helplessly.

The above review of the factors and conditions that contribute to reading problems has been, by no means, exhaustive. Limited space makes it impossible to mention all the probable causes of reading retardation, but it is hoped that some of the more commonly found factors and their relationship to the learning of reading have been highlighted. The causes of reading problems are usually multiple in nature. A different combination of factors and conditions for any child might easily mean that he might have avoided difficulties in learning to read. The causes may be inherent within the child himself or manifest in his environment. They often include factors and conditions that are physiological, psychological, intellectual, or instructional in nature. Fortunately, most children, regardless of the cause or causes of their difficulties, can overcome their reading problems when they are given appropriate instruction by teachers trained in the teaching of reading skills.

3

Kinds of Reading Problems

ALTHOUGH many children experience difficulty in learning to read, most of them can and do learn when they are provided with adequate remedial instruction. This instruction must be given at the children's functioning level of achievement, it must provide teaching in the specific reading skills in which the children are deficient, and it must take into consideration any factors and conditions that may impede learning. If it does these things, children, in most instances, will make progress.

Appropriate instruction is based on those needs identified through accurate diagnosis. Diagnosis includes the systematic investigation of all possible causes contributing to a reading problem. It also involves a thorough appraisal of the pupil's reading capacities and an identification of his specific deficiencies. In addition, diagnostic measures attempt to determine what will be the most effective methods of teaching. When a thorough diagnosis has been completed, a program of instruction can be developed which will enable the child to overcome his reading deficiencies and permit him to read at a level commensurate with his mental capabilities.

If a child exhibits deficiencies in identifying printed words, his instruction should include the teaching of the word-recognition skills in which he is deficient. At the same time, visual-skills activities designed to strengthen visual retention, such as tachistoscopic drill, can be introduced. A child who cannot identify printed words easily and efficiently cannot be expected to read anything independently, no matter how simple the material. Children with word-recognition problems usually lack the skills necessary to phonetic and structural analysis, and these skills must be learned. Children must be able to respond correctly to the letters that represent all the single consonant sounds, the consonant blends and digraphs, the long and short vowel sounds, and the diphthongs. They need to become familiar with the conditions under which consonants and vowels may be silent, and when and how certain consonants control the sounds of vowels. They also need to learn how to divide words into syllables and how to locate accent correctly. They must also learn to work with compound words, root words, prefixes and suffixes, and contracted and abbreviated words.

Many children also need to be taught how to utilize configuration clues, picture clues, and meaning clues and how to use the dictionary as an aid in determining the pronunciation of words. Children should know how to use all available techniques in conjunction with each other. For them to rely exclusively on any one technique is bound to limit their development.

Some children can identify isolated words adequately, but they fail to derive much meaning from their reading. The instruction they require is different from that mentioned above. Some of these children do not know the meaning of enough words to gain understanding of what they read or hear. Their

30

speaking vocabularies must be enriched and extended. Other children know the meaning of specific words out of context but cannot grasp ideas that are expressed by words in sentences and paragraphs. They must learn to identify relationships and to make associations. Still other children are able to understand the literal meaning of what they read but are unable to grasp the implied meanings or to evaluate what they read. These children must be taught to reason, to relate the ideas on the printed page to their experience, information, and knowledge. They also must learn to react intelligently to the materials they read. Understanding reading materials involves many different skills, and instruction needs to be given in specific areas if deficiencies are to be overcome and reading problems solved.

In the middle and upper grades in school, good study habits and efficient reading skills become important. By the time a child reaches high school, they are mandatory. Academic competition increases each year as college entrance approaches. The pupils with efficient study habits and skills have a decided advantage over those with inefficient ones. The keys to the success of the good student are undoubtedly good reading and study habits and skills.

In order to be a fluent reader, a student must have a flexible reading approach. He should be able to read rapidly when he needs to and to read slowly and carefully when the occasion demands thoroughness. Unfamiliar and difficult material will not be read as rapidly as familiar and easy material. The purpose for which any reading is done helps determine reading speed. If the reader wants only to get a general impression or the main ideas of a selection, he can read quite rapidly. If, however, his purpose is to master all the details that are included in the selection, he must read the same selection with closer concentration. Nor is it essential that all the words of a selection be read. Pupils must be taught to read selectively;

31

that is, to read only the portions of the material that are relevant and important and to skip over unimportant and unnecessary parts. They must be taught to identify key words and phrases easily, to distinguish major ideas from minor details, and to spot clue words that indicate a shift in the direction of a discussion. Only as they do these things will they become fluent and efficient readers.

Efficiency in study requires more than the development of good habits, such as setting aside specific time for study, eliminating all kinds of distractions, and providing good lighting and not too comfortable chairs. Efficiency also requires skill in interpreting and following directions, in locating information, in evaluating and selecting factual data, and in organizing and retaining ideas and concepts. These skills are the hallmarks of a good student and of a scholar. A pupil who is equipped with proficient study skills derives the greatest returns from the time and energy spent on study.

A diagnosis of reading performance investigates all these aspects of reading and study and pinpoints areas of deficiency. Progress will be possible only when instruction is provided to overcome the weaknesses and deficiencies that exist. Increasing a pupil's reading speed will not enable him to identify words more accurately if he is deficient in word recognition. He will simply be taught to go nowhere fast. Only instruction in the specifics of word recognition will enable him to make improvement in this area. Likewise, instruction in word recognition will not necessarily be reflected in gains in greater understanding or in study skills if deficiencies exist in those areas. Reading is not a generalized unitary skill. It is a highly complex process made up of a large number of interrelated subskills, and teaching must be provided at each subskill level. Instruction must be specific and must be directed toward specific areas of deficiency.

Most children acquire all the reading skills as a routine

part of their normal instruction in their regular classrooms. Once a child falls behind in reading for any reason and begins to accumulate reading deficiencies, his teacher may find it very difficult to provide him with the individual instruction he needs as part of her routine instructional responsibilities. Limitations are often placed on teachers by curriculum requirements, administrative organization, and scheduling and grouping practices. As a result, the problem reader falls further and further behind unless special efforts are made by the school or by his parents to provide him with the required instruction.

Many schools at the present time offer remedial-reading services as an ongoing part of their daily program. In some instances, regular classroom teachers render remedial services before or after school hours. In other cases, reading specialists who have had training in the diagnosis and correction of reading problems are added to the staff of the school, and they offer remedial services during regular school hours. Remedial instruction is discontinued as soon as the pupil's problems are overcome and he can manage to keep up with his class.

In addition to the special reading services offered by the schools themselves, special instruction in reading is available from reading clinics. Many colleges and universities, particularly those which train reading specialists, have reading clinics in which diagnosis and instruction are available for nominal fees. Most of the larger cities also have a number of private reading clinics.

It is not at all uncommon for high schools to provide reading-improvement programs for all their students, even the better ones. All pupils can thus bring their reading skills to superior levels in order that they may function to the limit of their capacities. These courses are apt to focus attention on the development of specific study skills that are relevant to the content areas of the curriculum.

Regardless of the origin of the reading services, all reading programs attempt to accomplish the same purposes. Their primary concern is to raise pupils' reading achievement to effective levels as quickly as possible. In doing so, they use many of the materials that are used in the regular classroom. But in addition, reading programs frequently employ special materials and equipment. Mechanical devices, when used appropriately, can be helpful in encouraging and establishing good reading habits and skills.

The important thing to remember when using any mechanical reading aids, though, is that the instruments do not teach the skills of reading; they merely help in establishing some of the habits necessary to fluent reading. Reading is essentially a cerebral process and as such, is accomplished when the brain responds to the stimuli received through the sense organs. The perception of the stimuli may be enhanced through the use of mechanical devices, but the skills themselves must be taught, so that they are understood and consciously applied by the pupils. They cannot be mechanically instilled by an instrument.

The successful treatment of reading problems, then, depends upon accurate diagnosis of the difficulties a child may be having and the application of appropriate instructional methods for overcoming these difficulties. As indicated, the causes of reading retardation are complex. We would be naive if we assumed that the problems that exist could be conquered through the use of simple and easy methods.

PART II

Case Studies of Problem Readers

Introduction to Case Studies

THE case studies which follow are actual case histories that have been selected from the files of a reading clinic as examples of several different kinds of reading problems and problem readers. Only the names of the pupils have been changed; all other information pertaining to the case histories is real and true. Test scores are accurately reported and events are recorded as they happened.

In each instance, the pupil's age and school-grade placement at the time of referral to the reading clinic is indicated. Each pupil was administered a standardized reading test as a part of his diagnosis before any remedial instruction was initiated. All pupils were also administered parallel forms of their original reading tests at the termination of their instructional periods to measure their progress. In some instances, tests were likewise given at various points during the instructional period or several months after instruction was terminated. Frequently it happens that a period of time is required for the adequate assimilation of learning before any measurable gains are reflected in increased test scores. Reference is made in the case studies to tests given at these several different times.

The purposes of diagnosing reading problems include the

37

identification of factors and conditions that may have contributed to reading failure and that may still be interfering with learning. They also include a complete evaluation of reading to determine the pupil's instructional reading level (the level at which he will profit most from instruction and which therefore should be used for teaching purposes) and to identify specific areas of weakness in reading skills. In addition, one of the purposes of diagnosis is to plan corrective procedures in the light of the obtained information.

To accomplish all these purposes, many different instruments and techniques are used to collect the necessary evidence. A variety of formal and informal tests may be used, questionnaires and inventories may be utilized as needed, and interviews may be arranged with relevant people. Information may also be solicited from school records as well as reports from pediatricians, ophthalmologists, psychologists, psychiatrists, and any other specialists who may have had contact with the pupil under consideration. Only by studying the pupil's reading problem against the background of as much information as may be obtained, is it possible to make intelligent decisions concerning corrective or remedial measures.

There is no one formula or prescribed procedure for the diagnosis of reading problems. In diagnosing as well as in correcting reading problems, some people place emphasis on some things and other people place emphasis on other things, depending upon their background, training, and previous experience. This is just as true in other fields, such as medicine, where one doctor may consider supplementary vitamins very important and another doctor may consider them useless and unnecessary. Both doctors, however, may be equally successful in their medical practices. In general, all reading specialists, as all doctors, agree on fundamental principles, although they may differ on details. The important thing is that despite these differences in personal philosophies and frames of reference, specialists generally succeed in helping retarded readers overcome their reading problems.

The pupils described in the succeeding pages were all diagnosed at the reading clinic before remedial instruction was initiated. In most instances, the pupils were given standardized reading achievement tests to assess their status in reading. Observation of their behavior while taking the tests also revealed important information about their problems. Many of them were also given informal textbook tests to identify specific deficiencies in word recognition, understanding, and fluency in reading. They were all given dominance tests to determine the possible existence of laterality confusion, since it is believed by many reading specialists that the lack of consistent laterality may interfere not only with the establishment of adequate directional habits in reading but also with the development of all facets of language. Tachistoscopic tests were given to assess visual skills, since fluent reading is highly dependent upon efficient visual performance. In addition, all pupils were personally interviewed to reveal their attitudes and feelings toward their reading problems. Their parents were also interviewed to secure background information concerning the etiology of the problem, to determine parental attitudes and feelings toward the child and his problems, and to impress the parents with the importance of their cooperation and assistance in helping to overcome the child's difficulties. Whenever possible, interviews were also scheduled with school personnel, usually the child's classroom teacher or guidance counselor, to gain the benefit of their reactions and insights. If additional information was obtained in relation to any of the pupils as part of their diagnoses, it is reported in their case studies.

Each of the following case histories also reports a description of the remedial instruction that was provided and a report of the progress that was achieved by each pupil. Instruction was planned for each pupil in light of the particular difficulties that were revealed by the diagnosis. There is no implication here that other methods and procedures would not have succeeded. These case reports simply describe what was actually done in these cases. It is widely recognized that there are many different approaches to remedial teaching; emphasis is given to those facets of instruction which are considered important by the person doing the teaching. By and large, success is achieved by most people if instruction is directed toward specific areas of deficiency in reading regardless of the various emphases fostered and the different methods and techniques used.

The pupils described in the following case studies were taught word-recognition skills if they exhibited difficulties in identifying printed words, meaning skills if they failed to understand adequately what they read, techniques of fluency if they read slowly and laboriously, and study skills and methods for preparing and taking various types of tests and examinations, where help in these areas was indicated. Many different procedures and materials were used to accomplish these purposes. In some instances, regular reading books, trade books, textbooks, and workbooks were used. The tachistoscope, eye-movement accelerator, and reading pacer were used where their use was appropriate. Writing in notebooks and on the blackboard was carried on as needed by particular pupils.

Sometimes the pupils were instructed individually and sometimes in groups, depending upon the problems they exhibited and the arrangements that could be made at the time they received their instruction. In each instance, however, the instructional program was carefully planned for each child in the light of his particular deficiencies and altered in the light of the progress he made.

It will be noted that the pupils described in the final two case studies are not retarded readers in the usual sense, since their reading achievement does not fall below their grade level.

However, not all problem readers score below grade level on reading tests. Tests are not always comprehensive measures of all reading skills. Therefore, it is possible for a pupil to score well on a reading test and still suffer from serious deficiencies in reading in those areas not tapped by the test.

Many pupils who score at grade level on reading tests are capable of far greater achievement with respect to their intellectual development. For example, a twelve-year-old pupil in the sixth grade with an IQ of 150 who scores only at a sixth-grade level is not realizing his potentialities at all. He is actually more retarded in reading than a sixth-grade pupil with an average IQ who scores only at a fourth- or fifth-grade level. Pupils who score well on tests still may have reading problems and can profit from special reading instruction. With a little help, these average achievers can easily become superior achievers in school. An inefficient reader cannot be an effective student.

The case studies that follow provide portraits of pupils who, at many different age and grade levels, experienced many different kinds of reading problems for many different reasons. These case histories are not intended to represent definitive and complete studies of the relationship between reading deficiencies and specific causative factors. Nor are they intended to delineate the only possible methods for overcoming reading problems. Rather, their purpose is to provide some descriptions and indications of the kinds of problems many children face in trying to succeed in school. It is also hoped that they will provide some suggestions for what may be done to help children with reading problems.

Section A—General Obstacles to Learning

Many children encounter difficulties in learning to read. The sources of their difficulties often defy accurate diagnosis, although in many such cases, an underlying emotional insecurity may be present. This insecurity may be of such a generalized nature, however, that its cause cannot be identified with sufficient certainty to help the conscientious teacher. When confronted with a student who should, by all standards, be making progress, but is not, the teacher's only available approach is the application of ordinary teaching techniques, including basic phonic and visual training. Students in this category are often regarded by their teachers and parents, without any real evidence, as "immature" or "confused" or low in "IQ." To identify difficulties in these vague terms serves no constructive purpose. The underlying causes for these symptoms, if ascertainable, can be helpful in providing a fruitful diagnosis; however, such identification may often require a depth analysis not warranted by the degree of difficulty encountered. These students can usually be successfully taught basic reading skills through a logical and coherent instructional program. The case histories that follow exemplify children who fall into this category.

Case Study 1

Student: **Stephen B.**

Age: **8**

School Grade: **3 (Beginning of Grade 3)**

Initial Reading Score: **Gr. 2.2 ***

Hours of Instruction: **42**

Diagnosis

Stephen experienced great difficulty while taking a reading test. Sitting still for the length of time required was next to an impossible task for him. The test results showed him to be reading at a level equivalent to the second month of the second grade. He possessed no phonic attack; in fact, his knowledge of phonics was limited to the sounds associated with about three-fourths of the consonants of the alphabet. He had no knowledge of the vowel sounds. Visual retention was weak, and his spelling, even of the most common words, had little relation to the words themselves. While taking the test, Stephen worked for a minute, got out of his chair, chewed his pencil, looked at the ceiling, squatted on his heels, and then looked

* Scores achieved on tests are reported in grade equivalents. A score of 2.2 is equivalent to the achievement of the average pupil in the second month of the second grade. A score of 4.3 would mean the achievement of an average pupil in the third month of the fourth grade, and so on.

around for someone to talk to. He behaved like a child three years younger than he was. Stephen's score on the test was something of a surprise, since, from his activities while being tested, it was expected that he would achieve practically nothing. But he had evidently gained a fleeting familiarity with a sufficient number of words to make correct guesses about some of the questions. He relied primarily on scattered clues, since he possessed too little knowledge to use systematic reading skills.

Stephen tested out as right-handed and right-footed, but he sighted with either his left or his right eye indiscriminately. His co-ordination was not abnormally poor but neither was it smooth and efficient. When Stephen walked, he covered an erratic course. He seemed almost to sweep along in a straight run, then to relax into a loose-limbed, sidewise, slouching walk. His hands and arms flapped out at his sides and his elbows stuck away from his body. When Stephen was called to attention and told to walk properly and use an even gait, the eccentricities of his movement disappeared and he walked with reasonable evenness. It was difficult to determine whether the erratic motion was simply disorganized childish energy or whether it had a more profound source.

When he wrote, Stephen formed his letters surprisingly well. There was no jerkiness to his writing and his letters were not peaked or jagged. He seemed to have achieved small muscle control consistent with his age. Whatever evidence was available seemed to point to the fact that by making a direct effort under close supervision, Stephen was capable of achieving normal performance. The tentative conclusion reached was that Stephen had retained, to an excessive degree, certain of the motion patterns of his earlier years and had developed a habit of exaggerating the more bizarre elements in this pattern in order to distract adults. Such distraction could serve to hide the inadequacies which he subconsciously might believe were his.

The mixed dominance identified in Stephen was not as severe as in many cases. He showed only a small tendency to left-sidedness. He did not use his left hand more than was usual in a right-handed person. On the tachistoscopic test, he performed reasonably well for his level and reversals were not frequent. Although Stephen demonstrated laterality confusion, it was not of a severe order.

Conference with Schoolteacher

Stephen's teacher reported that while he tested high on the intelligence tests administered by the school, his achievement was well below capacity. She described him as a dreamer with a short attention span. She said he did not sit still in class and was easily distracted. She felt that if some way could be found to hold his attention, he would have little difficulty in learning the basic reading skills; however, most of her time with him was spent in disciplining him. She had concluded that he was too immature to learn, and she felt very little could be done with him until he grew up. She had tried to understand the reasons for his refusal to accept the responsibilities consistent with his age. She believed that he was clinging to an infantile pattern of conduct in order to excuse himself from accepting his responsibility. She said that his parents were overprotective and that he manipulated them cleverly by insisting, through his actions, that he was too young to do his schoolwork. She reported that he would occasionally lapse into baby talk and that she reprimanded him severely when he did so. He was capable of speaking intelligently for his age, but he demanded the attention he could gain by behaving like a four-year-old.

Stephen's teacher had been concerned about his difficulty, but her patience had worn thin and had been replaced by hostility. She said she realized that she was now unable to work effectively with the boy and had requested that he be removed from her class. She felt that a man teacher might have better success with Stephen. She regretted that the situation had reached the point it had, but she felt it was kinder to Stephen for her to accept the facts realistically. The whole question of Stephen had been complicated for her by the fact that she had always found him a very attractive child and that she became upset when her insistence on his performing school activities made him unhappy. His ability to charm adults, while at the same time annoying them, had made it particularly difficult for her to achieve any measure of success with him.

Conference with Parent

Stephen's mother was a very attractive woman in her late twenties. She was puzzled and confused over Stephen's academic difficulties. She insisted that he seemed to grasp things very quickly. She said he was often very helpful and co-operative at home. Stephen had two younger brothers. His mother realized that he had to compete for her attention, but she said that she devoted twice as much time to Stephen as she did to the other two boys. She reported that Stephen's father had little patience with the boy, calling him babyish. Stephen's father would rarely take the boy with him when he went anywhere.

Stephen's mother was questioned closely regarding his mixed-dominance tendencies. She said that he had shown some confusion at an early age about which hand to use, but the family doctor had assured her that this was normal.

Stephen's mother was asked to encourage Stephen to use his right hand in all activities. It was suggested that he also be encouraged to learn to shoot a BB gun under his father's tutelage. It was explained that he should aim with his right eye and he should be encouraged to sight with that eye as much as possible. It was also explained to her that some authorities would go so far as to recommend that Stephen wear a patch over his left eye, but such a course seemed extreme.

Stephen's speech, his mother was told, required continuous attention. If he used baby talk, he should be corrected immediately. It was suggested that he spend a good deal of time with adults and be spoken to, by them, as though he were an adult himself. In order to extend his vocabulary and his familiarity with more advanced words, both parents should develop the habit of teaching him to be more observant. He should be asked to comment on the things he saw about him. He should be taken on walks and on rides in the car and asked questions about things that came into view. The questions should encourage him to think in verbal terms. He should be encouraged to express his thoughts. If, for instance, while walking they were to pass a store window, he should be asked to identify the objects in the window, to tell what they were for, to describe the objects by telling their color and what they were made of. It was pointed out that such activities were helpful in the development of maturity and of verbal skills.

Stephen's mother said that his teacher had told her that Stephen's immature conduct was being used by him to excuse his unwillingness to learn, and she wondered what could be done to overcome this problem. It was pointed out to her that the boy was probably clinging to his immature conduct because he felt unable to cope with the comparatively complex world of school. He seemed to lack confidence in his ability to meet the challenges that his schoolwork offered. It would be necessary to convince him that he had the capacity for succeeding before he could be expected to accept his responsibilities.

The pattern of failure experienced by Stephen every day in school had probably started because of the difficulty he encountered in retaining an accurate image of first, letters and numbers, and then, words. The mixed-dominant tendency, which is usually accompanied by faulty visual retention, would account in large measure for this difficulty. Feeling unable to compete with his classmates, he had probably fallen into a routine of emphasizing infantile elements in his behavior. This routine might well have stemmed initially from the need to compete against his younger brothers for attention.

Stephen's mother was told that these judgments were superficial and were offered only to give her something to think about. If, however, Stephen's performance continued unchanged, she would be wise to seek the help of a competent psychologist.

Conference with Student

No conference as such was held with Stephen. He was, however, observed closely while initial instruction was being provided. Stephen's case had been thoroughly discussed with his instructor at the clinic, and from the outset, Stephen was made to understand that he would be expected to pay close attention. The teaching activities were, initially, to be changed every five minutes. Stephen seemed able to follow what was going on for about two or three minutes at a time, and then only while the instructor's eyes were on his face. He was asked whether or not he wanted to learn how to read, and he replied that he didn't. He said that it was hard and he did not want to learn. He was asked whether he would like to write on the blackboard. At this he grew animated, and jumped up for a piece of chalk. He began drawing wild lines, holding the chalk in his right hand. He was asked to print certain letters. He printed them two-feet high, and then erased them violently, holding the eraser in his left hand. He was asked to write them with his left hand and had difficulty holding the chalk, which squeaked on the board. Stephen evidently enjoyed performing before others. When he was asked to return to his seat, he had to be told a few times before he relinquished the chalk and eraser and sat down.

He was asked to read aloud from a first-grade reader. He complained that there were no pictures in the book. He was unable to read, so he was asked to point out words which he knew. He glanced at the print for about thirty seconds, then looked up and said he couldn't do it. He was told that he could be taught how to read, but he turned his eyes away and began to dig his pencil into his desk.

Recommendations

It would be necessary for Stephen to engage in activities in which he would experience some measure of success before he could be motivated sufficiently to put forth any effort. He had enough intelligence to grasp phonic principles, and basic phonics (taught primarily at the blackboard where he could participate actively by doing the writing) would provide an opportunity for successful achievement under conditions which were attractive to him.

Tachistoscopic exercises also held promise of providing an activity in which he could experience success. Initially, he would be asked to write on the blackboard the simple images flashed on the screen. His instructor was told that since, at this level, the most fruitful learning experiences were those gained through kinesthetic drill, Stephen was to be provided with activities which included his physical participation. It was felt that he had developed beyond the stage at which cut-out letter blocks might prove useful; however, they could be relied upon for help in teaching him the vowel sounds, since his knowledge of vowels was so slight. In all Stephen's training, his instructor was advised that emphasis should be placed on building left-to-right directional habits. The order in which letters appeared was to be scrupulously observed, and Stephen was to correct immediately any of his reversals or transpositions. Once basic word-attack skills were achieved, Stephen could then strive for fluency.

Instruction Provided

Phonic training was started immediately by concentrating on the letters of the alphabet and the sounds they made. After a fairly short period, Stephen began to respond to the large amount of individual attention he was receiving. He needed reassurance with every step he took, and the instructor was always at his elbow in order to provide it. He was first taught the vowel sounds, which were then identified within short words. Stephen had difficulty in grasping the concept that each letter, or combination of letters, made a sound of its own. He tended to regard the complete word as an entity in itself instead of seeing it as a number of related parts. He had also developed the habit of identifying the initial sounds of a word and guessing at the rest. At the same time that the idea of sounding out words was being brought home to Stephen, he was being taught not to sound each syllable separately but to try to relate the parts of a word to each other in his mind. The application of his phonic knowledge was made, from the start, a silent process. In this way, it was hoped that the habit of vocalizing could be avoided. Stephen was taught to identify the initial sound of a word, to isolate and identify the vowel sounds, and then to say the word as a whole. By concentrating on the vowel sounds, he was made, inevitably, to think about the structure of the word in syllables.

Stephen slumped in his chair, yawned, and twisted his head around; but by changing the activity and the instruction routine every few minutes, the instructor saved him from boredom. After fifteen hours of instruction, Stephen was able to

50

sound out simple words, and some of his attention-getting activities disappeared.

Meanwhile, tachistoscopic work and constant writing on the blackboard had familiarized Stephen with a number of words, and his sight vocabulary began to grow. Habits of visual retention were being built, and it was noted that, whereas, at first, he had to encounter a word a number of times in various contexts before he would remember it, he now was recalling words which he had encountered only a few times. Stephen was developing habits of *accurate seeing*. His mind was beginning to respond to what his eyes saw. At the same time, the habit of inattentiveness which had interfered with his reading development, was being overcome. When a tachistoscopic image was flashed on the screen, it was necessary for him to identify it immediately. This training taught him not to allow his mind to wander, and he began to be conscious of what his eyes were seeing.

Particularly with Stephen, the tachistoscope proved valuable, largely because it was a projection machine which threw a bright light on the screen and commanded his attention. The mechanical action of the device heightened the excitement of the activity, and Stephen's attentiveness was heightened too. He became very anxious to perform the tachistoscopic drills, and it was found that after a time he was able to engage in this activity for ten to twelve minutes at a time without letting his attention wander.

Initially, the tachistoscopic targets flashed for Stephen were very simple, consisting of two or three digits or letters. When, after a few weeks, he was able to identify four digits, he grew encouraged and began to feel that learning to read was within his grasp.

The pattern of failure which had grown so familiar to Stephen was beginning to be reversed. Along with the small successes achieved on the tachistoscope, Stephen was gaining the visual capacity for more accurate and comfortable performance of visual tasks. At about this time phonic exercises were combined with the tachistoscopic drills. Short words were flashed on the screen and Stephen was encouraged to analyze them according to the phonic principles he had been learning on the blackboard. The sight exercises and phonic analysis were combined into a single activity. The phonic analysis helped establish, too, the habit of seeing a word in its proper left-to-right direction, since the syllables had to be attacked in the correct order. Once some degree of skill in word attack had been achieved, eye-movement exercises were introduced. The instructor wrote a three- or four-line sentence on the blackboard. The sentence was read silently by Stephen as the instructor traced the sentence with the pointer, from left to right, smoothly. Once a reasonable degree of fluency had been acquired, Stephen was ready to work at slow speeds on the eye-movement acceleration device.

Bit by bit, painfully at times, Stephen began to develop both word-attack skills and fluency. He was still easily distracted and unable to concentrate for more than a few minutes at a time, but progress had been made and most important of all, he had finally accepted the fact that reading was possible for him.

Stephen's spelling, although often inaccurate, now at least had some logical relation to the words he was trying to spell. His handwriting, while never bad, showed dramatic improvement. The constant printing of letters had given him extensive practice.

Progress Achieved

By the time Stephen had completed forty-two hours of instruction, he was able to read easy third-grade material on his own. He was not a fluent or competent reader, but he had sufficient control over the necessary tools to enable him to tackle most of the work he would encounter. His terminal reading test score was Grade 3.7. His mother was told that it would be necessary for Stephen to read under supervision for at least fifteen minutes every day in order to insure retention of his gains, but it was felt that a breakthrough had been made, and it could be expected that as his skills grew, his confidence would also develop, and the immature behavior pattern, many elements of which he had already begun to drop, could be expected to change.

During the time that Stephen attended the clinic, he had been working with a man teacher in school. The combined pressures of special work at the clinic, plus a man at school whom he wished to please, had enabled Stephen to take a long step forward, and there was every expectation that he would continue to grow.

Case Study 2

Students: William and George S. (Identical Twins)

Ages: 8½

School Grade: 2 (Middle of Grade 2)

Initial Reading Score: Gr. 1.2

Hours of Instruction: 80

Diagnosis

The level of reading skill possessed by William and George S. was too low to be measured by standardized tests. They were nonreaders but had some familiarity with the names of about half the letters of the alphabet, although they were unable to identify these letters consistently when they saw them. They both were able to print a few letters but could not assign the proper names to these letters. Both boys had attended school for two-and-a-half years (excluding kindergarten). They had been retained in the second grade, and at the time they attended the clinic, were completing the first semester of second grade work for the second time. During the period of their school life, they seemed to have absorbed scarcely any academic knowledge. An attempt was made to test their knowledge of simple arithmetic. Their level of achievement in computation skills was about equal to their verbal knowledge. They were able to draw some single-digit numbers but were unable to name these numbers with accuracy.

A simple story of second-grade difficulty was read aloud to the twins, and they were asked questions to test retention. William was able to tell what the story was about in very general terms; George remembered the name of one of the characters, but it was obvious that their attention had wandered while the story was being read, and their grasp of the story was fragmentary. They were then asked to define commonly used words orally. They knew that the word "little" meant "small," but the word "large" drew no response from them. "Tall," William said, was "big," "water" was something you "drank," and "hard" was "like the floor." Although this sort of vocabulary test afforded no measurable evidence of verbal development, the impression gained was that their understanding of words was equivalent to that of an average five-year-old child. The verbal deficiency exhibited by both twins extended to their speech. They formed their words clumsily, slurring them together. They expressed themselves in brief phrases and half-formed sentences. The speech pattern of both was remarkably similar, although George had a tendency, when pressed for an answer to a simple question, to stutter slightly. When they spoke words, they would substitute one sound for another. It was difficult, for instance, to determine whether in saying a particular word they had meant a *b* or a *v* sound or whether they had made a *t* or a *d* sound. Auditory discrimination had been developed to only a slight degree.

Although both boys moved heavily, indicating that their physical co-ordination was not well developed, they still appeared to be within normal range. The dominance test revealed no evidence of lack of unilaterality; both were right-handed, right-footed, and right-eyed.

Conference with Psychologist

Both boys had been referred to the school's psychologist for diagnosis. She reported that according to her testing, William gave evidence of slightly higher basic intelligence than George. William's IQ score was seventy-five with a potential of ninety-one whereas George's was only three points lower. The psychologist regarded them both as being slightly retarded. However, since the parents of the boys had not been willing to allow the psychologist to undertake the exhaustive testing she felt was indicated, she advised that her test results were not to be accepted as completely reliable and final.

The parents were confused and upset by her findings, she said, and felt that lengthy diagnostic procedures might have an adverse effect on the twins. When asked whether she suspected physiological damage to the brain, the psychologist said there was always a suspicion of such a condition; however, without neurological evidence, it was impossible to know for sure. On the other hand, she said, certain environmental factors seemed to have had a particularly negative effect in this instance.

Twins frequently develop a private means of communication between themselves which enables them to exclude the rest of the world—at least in the early years of their lives. The necessity which most people feel to communicate with others is sometimes satisfied for twins by their almost automatic perception of what is in the other's mind. As a result, some pairs of twins fail to develop adequate verbal skills.

The psychologist described the case of another set of identical twins who were now adults. They had been brought up in an isolated mountain area in the state of Washington. Their contact with other human beings was infrequent, and when they did meet other children, they were usually youngsters from a nearby Indian reservation. These twins developed a fairly complete language of their own which was composed of fragments of English and Indian speech, liberally sprinkled with esoteric sounds of their own invention. Although both of these twins had high native intelligence, they did not achieve effective verbal skills. In their studies, they concentrated on nonverbal subjects, and eventually both of them became engineers, with Masters' degrees. But their dependence upon one another continued, since satisfactory communication was possible for them only with each other. At the age of thirty-five, they had never been separated from one another for more than a few days at a time.

The case of William and George, however, the psychologist added, was complicated by low intellectual development as well as by the underlying unwillingness on the part of the parents to recognize the problem realistically. A program of reading training, the psychologist felt, might prove helpful, but she doubted that the limited capacity of the twins would enable them to make substantial progress.

Conferences with Schoolteachers

The school attended by William and George had wisely assigned them to different classes. Both boys had conscientious teachers who were genuinely concerned about the academic problems encountered by the twins, and both teachers had devoted a good deal of their own time to working individually with them. However, the teachers were discouraged by the apparent lack of results gained through their efforts. They both felt that an extended program of individual attention would provide the only hope of teaching the boys to read. William's teacher said that working with him was often frustrating, except that it was also rewarding at times, since he would occasionally show unexpected signs of progress. His understanding of what she taught him was poor, but with repetition, she found that certain basic principles would eventually be grasped, and once William had the knowledge, she could rely on him to retain it. George's teacher, on the other hand, reported that his retentive powers were very weak. At times he would seem to understand and grasp what he was taught and to remember it throughout the entire period of instruction, but the next day his recollection of his knowledge was nonexistent.

Neither teacher subscribed completely to the judgment of the school psychologist. They both reported having received a report about the boys from the psychologist, but they felt that the prognosis was not as negative as the report indicated. William's teacher remarked that she felt that the undeveloped verbal skills of the boys made accurate evaluation of intelligence close to impossible, and she seemed to feel that once the boys had achieved sufficient verbal dexterity to express their ideas, they would begin to perform within a normal range of intelligence.

Both teachers were pleased that the boys were to receive special individual instruction in reading, and both asked that they be kept closely informed of the training provided and that progress reports on the boys' achievements be furnished to them. William's teacher particularly requested that the clinic advise her of the specific instruction that the boys were receiving, so that she might supplement it at school.

Conference with Parent

Mrs. S. was worried and depressed about the report she had received from the school psychologist. Although she had realized all along that the twins were in difficulty, she had felt it was only a passing phase. She said she was willing to do anything that held out hope of their learning to read, but she wondered whether or not their IQ scores were so low that reading would be beyond their capacity. It was pointed out to her that the teachers of the boys were hopeful that they would be able to achieve some measure of reading ability, although obviously they were handicapped. Mrs. S. complained that she could not understand why it had happened to her; her two other children were perfectly bright and were doing well enough in school. She said that she and her husband had done everything possible for the boys; they were sent to good camps in the summer, they had a swimming pool, they were taken in the car wherever they wanted to go, and in fact, they got whatever they wanted.

With regard to scheduling instruction periods for the twins, Mrs. S. had to juggle her busy social schedule to enable her to bring the youngsters to the clinic three afternoons a week after school. She murmured that the boys did not really appreciate what she had to do but added quickly that it was well worth it if the instruction taught them to read. Although the scholastic difficulties the twins were encountering represented a great inconvenience to Mrs. S., she was still genuinely concerned that an effective course be taken to help them overcome their problems. Mrs. S. was asked whether she or Mr. S. would be able to spend at least half an hour each night with the boys, going over drill exercises that would be provided. She was assured that specific instructions would be given to her. She said that Mr. S. was much too busy but that she would be able to work with them, even though she had found in the past that whenever she attempted to help them, she lost patience quickly. But now that she knew they had real handicaps, she felt that she would be able to work with them more successfully if she were given specific directions. She said they simply had to learn to read, and wondered aloud what sort of life they would make for themselves. She was told that in all probability they would develop sufficient academic skills to operate on a sufficiently high level to enable them to hold jobs and lead normal lives.

Conference with Students

The twins were given first-grade readers and asked to glance through them. There were few pictures in the books and William complained that he could not read. They were asked to look for any words that they might know; George identified the words "a" and "to"; William said he could not find any, and his eyes began wandering around the room—he had lost interest. George picked up a pencil and began to draw lines in the book. He was told to stop. Meanwhile, William's eyes had settled on a desk pen. He took it from its stand and began to scribble on the desk pad. He was relieved of the pen and both boys were talked to sternly. They responded by staring into space, their faces impassive. They were asked whether they wanted to learn to read. Neither answered. They were then asked if they liked school. William began to talk about his father's Cadillac, and George said he had the biggest swimming pool on the block. William told a story about a boy at school. When he spoke, he ran his words together, slurring the sounds, and it was very difficult to understand what he was saying. He was asked to repeat what he said about the boy at school, but by this time he had lost interest and was gazing at the telephone. George got up from his chair and started for the door. He was ordered to sit down, which he did reluctantly.

The erratic pattern of the twins' behavior was a preview of the difficulties that would be encountered in teaching them to read.

Recommendations

Although both boys had been exposed to some phonic training at school, neither had been able to grasp any of the basic principles. On the other hand, neither had they been able to develop more than a very limited sight vocabulary. It was decided that visual retention would have to be developed and that every possible aid would be employed. In particular, it was felt that kinesthetic and tactile experiences should be utilized along with visual and auditory experiences in order to give them the necessary primary knowledge. At the same time as work with letters was carried on, the sounds made by each letter would be repeated by the instructor and by the twins. The aim of the projected program would be to provide repetitive experience which would, however, be presented in activities that were as varied as possible. Instructional periods would be limited to one hour, each hour to be divided into approximately eight or ten different activity periods. Physical movement from one activity room to another was to be considered essential, since it reduced the likelihood of boring the boys. Activity sessions were to be made as active as possible. The boys were to be separated whenever feasible. Bit by bit, each of them was to be assigned simple tasks and left to himself for a period of three to four minutes to accomplish them. Lagging interest was to be the signal for a change of activity. Overall rigid control was to be exercised. The instructor was to insist on performance and was not to tolerate excessive interruptions or naughty and distracting behavior.

Instruction Provided

The instructor assigned to the twins was a man. He was a mature person, rather brusque in his manner. The first activity to which the twins were introduced involved working with cutout letter blocks. A few letters were selected. The instructor called out the name of a letter, then gave its sound. The boys were asked to find the letter. Once it had been found, they were to look at it and then print it in their notebooks. While printing the letter, they repeated its sound three times. From this activity they went immediately to the tachistoscopic room where the

61

same letters were flashed on the screen. Again they printed the letters in their notebooks, sounding them as they printed. From this room, they went to a small blackboard room where the instructor called out the names and sounds of letters, which the boys then wrote on the blackboard, sounding the letters as they printed. After six or eight letters had been printed by them on the blackboard, they returned to their seats and printed the letters in their notebooks, again saying the sounds. They next went to individual study cubicles where they opened their readers. The instructor called out the names and sounds of letters, and the boys located them in their readers. Once they had found a letter, they printed it in their notebooks and sounded it as they wrote. The instructor then took them to a table on which were large sheets of paper. While they printed large letters on the sheets of paper, the boys named the letters and their sounds and then printed them in their notebooks and sounded them. Within five or six hours of this kind of instruction, the twins knew the alphabet and knew the sounds made by all of the consonants and by some of the vowels. They now possessed the first phonic tools for reading.

The next step involved teaching them to put sounds together to form simple words. Initially, the names and sounds of three letters were called out. The twins had to find the cut-out letters and arrange them in the order in which the sounds were heard in the word spoken by the instructor. The boys then sounded the word, letter by letter; first the initial letter, then the vowel sound, and then the last letter. They then pronounced the word. They were able to sound the individual letters without too much difficulty, but blending the sounds together to form a word proved a serious obstacle. The three-letter words constructed out of the cut-out letters were then flashed for them on the tachistoscope. Again they printed these words in their notebooks, sounding them as they wrote.

For approximately twenty hours of instruction, the twins

worked with cut-out letters, the tachistoscope, blackboard, notebooks, large sheets of paper, and the first-grade readers which were being used to enable them to find and identify words in normal-printed context. By this time, they were able to sound out many simple words. The close attention they were forced to pay to each word helped them to retain the image of the word, and some headway was made in developing a sight vocabulary.

At the conclusion of another ten hours of instruction, the twins were able to read and write very simple sentences. The next step was to provide a broader experience with words. More specific and extensive instruction in the vowel sounds was now undertaken. Through repetition and insistence that each letter be printed and sounded, the beginning of a working knowledge of the vowels was achieved. At the same time, it was decided that the twins were ready to begin eye-movement training. Film-strip stories, first-grade level, were projected on the screen. A left-to-right masking mechanism, moving at a very slow pace, forced their eyes to follow the story. The wavering attention of the twins was most readily captured by the projection devices. Working in a semidarkened room and watching the brightly lit screen, the boys seemed able to focus their attention, and they were less easily distracted. Some of the excitement attendant on seeing a movie evidently carried over to this teaching situation with good effect.

Session by session, the boys began to build reading skills. They learned to rely on the phonic elements, which gave them a means of word attack. When they encountered a new word, they would automatically attempt to sound it out. At the same time, their sight vocabulary began to expand as they learned to examine each word carefully and to remember it.

From the beginning, the difficulty the boys found in pronouncing words accurately proved to be an additional problem. When they had sounded out a word properly, they would often not recognize it as a word in their own speaking vocabularies, since their pronunciation was so slurred. A good deal of time was spent in insisting that they pronounce each word distinctly, since only by so doing could they relate the letters to the sounds in words correctly.

Throughout the training, frequent conferences were held with the boys' mother, and telephone conversations with their teachers at school were a regular feature. Mrs. S. was told that it was important that the twins be included in adult conversation at home in order to extend their speaking vocabularies. They were also to be corrected when they pronounced words sloppily. She was to make a special effort to talk with the boys for extended periods each day and to arrange for them to meet with other people, both children and adults, for the purpose of conversing. She was asked, as well, to read aloud to the boys each night for at least half an hour, and when she complained that they would not sit still that long, it was pointed out to her that finding sufficiently interesting material at their level would help the situation. If they complained or rebelled, she was to be insistent, for it was essential that they expand their verbal experiences.

After sixty hours of instruction at the clinic, the twins were beginning to read first-grade material on their own. They understood reasonably well what they read. At this point it was decided that the twins were ready to concentrate on developing reading fluency and further extension of their vocabularies. A greater proportion of time was now devoted to working on the eye-movement accelerator, and the masking mechanism was gradually speeded up. In the beginning of this phase, the twins would read one sentence aloud; they would then read the following three sentences to themselves and the next one aloud. The machine was stopped and questions were immediately asked. Gradually, the number of sentences read silently was increased until an entire selection could be read by the boys to themselves.

The reading of the boys began to grow less halting. William, at this stage, was moving ahead more rapidly than George (up to this time, their progress had been comparable). During the early phase of the training, they had progressed at about the same rate, although one day one would spurt ahead, the next day the other. Their daily performance depended to a large extent upon what had happened to them during the time immediately preceding their attendance at the clinic, but as their reading skills began to grow more firm, their performance was more consistent and less dependent upon their emotional states.

Progress Achieved

George and William received eighty hours of special instruction over a period of about seven months. The instruction was not continuous; there were breaks for vacations or simply for the purpose of relieving the pressure.

Nationally standardized tests were administered at this time. George tested out two months below grade level and William two months above—their grade level being the end of the second grade at this time.

The teachers at school reported that both boys were participating in class activities. Although they were unable to work on their own consistently and their attention span was still very short, they at least were participating members of their classes. It was felt that they were finally benefitting from attendance at school. It was suggested to Mrs. S. that the twins be withdrawn from the clinic and it was arranged that they be brought back for testing six months later, so that their retention could be checked.

Case Study 3

Student: Deborah N.

Age: 10

School Grade: 4 (End of Grade 4)

Initial Reading Score: Gr. 2.7

Hours of Instruction: 50

Diagnosis

While taking the diagnostic test, Deborah exhibited strong signs of impatience with herself. She had been asked by the person administering the test to read a sentence or two aloud and had then been asked to identify certain printed words and some phonograms. On the basis of this cursory test procedure, it was decided that her reading level was too low to enable her to complete a fourth-grade test, and she was given instead a primary-level diagnostic test. She glanced over the entire page of test material before making a stab at the first question. She tried to answer a question in the proper manner by underlining a word, changed her mind, and then rather violently blacked out the entire word. Her eyes again darted over the page, almost desperately, as though she were seeking clues. She jumped from question to question. As soon as she felt herself stumped by a word, she moved on to the next question. Halfway through the next question, she went back to the original one. Her per-

66

formance indicated extreme anxiety and tension and lack of confidence. The test showed her to be working more than two years below level. Her knowledge of phonics was nonexistent. Her eye-movement pattern was scattered and ineffectual.

A story was read aloud to Deborah and she was asked specific questions about the characters and events depicted. While being read to, Deborah's attention wandered frequently. She was unable to answer many of the questions. Even the often-repeated names of some of the characters had not been retained by her. It was not only that her attention span was short; her powers of concentration had been disrupted. Deborah's school world was obviously a chaotic place, without coherence or logic; a world filled with fear. She was expected to perform a number of academic tasks and lacked the tools for accomplishing them. A close analysis of her test revealed some strange inconsistencies. She was unable to answer some of the most primary questions, but correctly completed some of the more difficult ones. Her sight vocabulary was a random accumulation of odds and ends of words which, for one reason or another, had stuck in her mind, but many of the most frequently encountered words had made no impression on her.

Deborah would have represented a far less difficult problem had she been innocent of any reading knowledge at all. As it was, the smattering of reading elements which she had grasped served only further to confuse and frustrate her.

Deborah tested out as a strong unilateral dominant. She was right-handed, right-eyed, and right-footed. Her physical coordination was excellent. She moved gracefully and easily, but when under tension, her hands doubled into fists and she walked stiffly. She was quite small for her age and looked at least two years younger than she actually was. Her handwriting was erratic and the letters were badly formed. She had great difficulty in staying on the line as she wrote. All of her sentences tended to curve downward toward the end of a line. Her writing was very black; she bore down heavily on her pencil while taking the diagnostic test, twice breaking the pencil point.

Conference with Schoolteacher

Her teacher said that Deborah had been at her present school for only two months. Her previous school had been in Texas and her records had not as yet been forwarded. The teacher had scarcely had time to become acquainted with Deborah, since the term was ending and the pressure of end-of-term work had been fairly heavy. She realized that Deborah was having difficulty in doing schoolwork. She said that the child had not made friends with any of the other children in her class. Since Deborah had been there so short a time, the teacher had attached no special significance to that. For the most part, Deborah came to school a minute before the late bell, sat at her desk, and had nothing to say. The teacher realized that the child's written work needed attention, but she was unaware that Deborah's reading level was so low. She said that the school would test the youngsters in September, which was only a few months away. Since Deborah's records were not available, the school had been reluctant to make any quick decisions as to the best way of handling her. The teacher candidly said that they had, therefore, allowed things to drift along with the intention of getting busy with Deborah when the new term started.

Conference with Parent

Deborah's mother came to the conference after having cancelled two previous appointments at the last minute. She was an attractive woman, full of nervous energy. She spoke rapidly with a deep, low-pitched voice. She said that she and her husband knew that Deborah was in trouble and that they had been meaning to do something about it for some time. Her husband was in the army and they had been stationed in many parts of the world. His assignments were usually brief. The longest stay at any one post had been the year they had spent in Germany when Deborah was in the second grade. Since that time, they had been stationed in Hawaii, Tennessee, Washington, D.C., and Texas. Deborah had been in service school in Germany and in Hawaii, although, for a period of five months in Germany, she had not attended school at all. It had taken them so long to get settled, and Deborah's mother had taken Deborah with her on side trips to Paris and Rome. The three of them (Deborah was an only child) had also spent a vacation in Madrid. In Hawaii, Deborah had attended an excellent school, and they had been sorry that she had not been able to spend more time there, but it had taken them two months to find a school. Also, there were the trips to the other islands which interfered with school attendance. She and her husband had always felt that whatever Deborah had lost in the way of formal schooling had been more than made up for in the interesting places and people she had encountered.

It was pointed out to Deborah's mother that the child had become seriously confused. She seemed anxious and resentful and was frustrated at not being able to perform her academic work. It was suggested that psychological help might well be sought, since it was felt that in her present frame of mind, Deborah would make slow progress with reading. Deborah's mother was intelligent. She said she felt that she understood the reasons why Deborah was so unsettled. They confidently expected to remain at their present location for three years and felt that in that time, they could do a great deal to help repair the damage done. They intended to give Deborah a more stable and secure home life. They had discussed the problem with a friend who was a psychiatrist and they were well aware of some of the underlying difficulties. In the mean-

69

time, she believed special work in reading would help Deborah to make the necessary adjustment. She and her husband had discussed the problem fully and were sure that with the guidance of their friend, the child would make progress.

She was asked whether she had any idea of the sort of reading training Deborah had received during her school life. She said that as far as she knew, most of the teachers had used a flash-card system, although in the school in Hawaii, Deborah had begun to bring home phonic exercises which required her to sound out words after breaking them into syllables. A great deal of attention had been paid at that time to her handwriting, and forming letters in a left-to-right direction was emphasized; however, the training started at this school had been brief. When they had been transferred from Hawaii to Tennessee, Deborah's new teacher, a young girl just out of normal school, had informed them that Deborah was not yet mature enough to learn to read, and little or nothing had been accomplished during their short stay there. Deborah's teacher in Texas had been a motherly woman who had been very fond of Deborah and had warned the parents not to put too much pressure on her.

Conference with Psychiatrist

Deborah's mother had furnished the name and telephone number of the psychiatrist with whom she and her husband had discussed Deborah's problem. He said he had known the family on and off for a number of years but that none of them had ever been patients of his, so that he could speak only in general terms. He reported that it was apparent that Deborah was upset emotionally as the result of not having been provided a stable home life. Her parents, although charming and intelligent people, had been neglectful. They had pursued their own activities with small consideration for the child and her needs.

Although he realized full well the pressures they were under—the father was a lieutenant colonel in the army and the social responsibilities of his position were great—as far as he knew, there had been no serious attempt by the parents to face the problem of Deborah's education. It had only been very recently that he had been able to convince them of the necessity of their thinking seriously about the child's emotional development. He said he was familiar with a number of cases of children whose families had moved around a good deal. In general, the only antidote to this nomadic sort of life, as far as the children's development was concerned, was a closely knit family group in which lavish displays of affection were common. Even in these families, the children seemed to be handicapped as compared with youngsters brought up in a more stable environment. Childhood, he said, seemed to require the constant reassurance provided by familiar surroundings and people.

Recommendations

It was felt that no good purpose could be served by conferring with Deborah. She needed encouragement and reassurance and this could best be provided while she was being taught.

The aim of any training for a student as confused as Deborah would be to simplify the steps necessary to the achievement of reading skills and to arrange these steps in as logical and orderly a sequence as possible. It was felt necessary that she be absolutely certain of the first step before being asked to grasp the second step. Basic phonics would be taught her initially. Tachistoscopic work would be used only for reinforcement of the phonic training. Practice in writing, while sounding the letters as she wrote, was considered essential. Constant encouragement would also be necessary in order to help Deborah establish the needed confidence. Once a beginning phonic attack had been established, concentration on visual discrimination would begin. The development of eye-movement habits would not be attempted until basic word-attack skills had been developed. Comprehension exercises would not be introduced until reasonable fluency had been achieved. In all training, it was felt that any sort of overt pressure should be avoided until after Deborah herself had begun to recognize her own ability.

Instruction Provided

Deborah came reluctantly for her instruction. She seemed to expect only further confusion. The first six hours of training were devoted largely to pointing out to Deborah how much she actually did know that would be useful in helping her to become a good reader. In her phonic training, she was impressed with the fact that she knew the names of the letters of the alphabet and the sounds of the consonants. It was pointed out to her that once she mastered the vowel sounds, she would be able to sound out most words. It was found that Deborah had difficulty with the blends. Deborah tended to sound a weak vowel between the two blended consonants, but her auditory discrimination was good and she quickly learned that the b-l blend did not say "bul" but was like the sound heard in the beginning of the word "blue." She was then taught that the *c* and *g* both have two sounds; a soft sound and a hard sound. When these letters were followed by an *e, i,* or *y,* they ordinarily made soft sounds; the *c* sounded like an *s* and the *g* like a *j.* Otherwise they made their hard sounds, the *c* sounding like *k* and the *g* like the *g* in goat. Deborah found this concept difficult to grasp. A good deal of time was spent on examples, and the tachistoscopic exercises for a number of days included the sounds of *c* and *g.*

She fared better with the consonant digraphs, since she already knew the *sh* and *ch* sounds. She tended to confuse *th* and *wh* until she had completed a number of exercises requiring a differentiation of these sounds, one from another.

An attempt was being made to provide Deborah with the basic phonic knowledge that she would need to read at her level. All complicated and exceptional elements were disregarded for the time being, and she was told that they could be learned as they arose. About this time two-syllable words were introduced. Deborah was taught that a syllable is the basic pronunciation unit of words and is dependent upon vowel sounds. The number of syllables in any word depended upon the number of vowel sounds in the word. A syllable, therefore, could consist of a vowel alone but not of a consonant alone.

At first, it was difficult for Deborah to isolate the vowel sounds, since she had never been asked to think about them. The instructor wrote *b—d* on the blackboard and had Deborah sound out the letters. He then asked Deborah if these sounds reminded her of any words. She said the word "bed," and when she was made aware that she also might make the words "bad" and "bud," she was on the way to recognizing what constituted a vowel sound. Deborah was delighted to discover she already knew the sounds of the long vowels, since they were identical with the names of the five vowel letters. Many exercises containing the long vowel sounds were done with her, and it was pointed out that there are two signals to look for in determining whether or not a vowel is long. One signal is the *e* at the end of the word and the second is another vowel immediately following the first. The *a,* she was told, is lengthened by an *i* immediately after it; the *e* by an *a,* and the *o* by an *a.* Deborah was introduced at this point to the short vowels. These represented a difficult problem for her, since the short vowel sounds are so similar to each other and so different from the letters they represent.

With the help of nonsense sentences ("That bed is not up.")

73

—each word of which contained a short vowel sound—she was taught to isolate and identify the short vowels. The instructor wrote the five vowels across the top of the blackboard. He then told Deborah a word with a short vowel sound and she was asked to write this word under the appropriate vowel.

In this way, she was taught to listen for the vowel sounds contained within specific words. It was necessary at first for her to say the word a few times before she could hear the vowel sound accurately and, for encouragement, she would point to one of the columns under the five vowels and look at the instructor to see whether she were on the right track. But after practice, she became more sure of herself and went unhesitatingly to the correct column. Having Deborah write on the blackboard effectively helped her to maintain a high level of interest. She became eager to do these exercises and often asked the instructor when they would do blackboard work.

When Deborah knew her short and long vowel sounds, exercises were introduced in which a short vowel word was changed to a long vowel word; thus "bat" was changed to "bait," and "hat" to "hate." Deborah was very pleased when this mystery was cleared up for her.

At this time, Deborah was taught a systematic procedure for sounding out words. She was taught to identify the initial consonant sounds, then the vowel sounds, and then she was asked to pronounce the words in their entirety. The aim was to teach her to think of the words under attack as a series of sounds and to say them as wholes. Only in that way could Deborah avoid the development of halting reading habits.

The vowels followed by *r* were next taught to Deborah. She was surprised to discover that *er, ir,* and *ur* make the same sound, but she was told that for spelling purposes, she would have to remember the appearance of a word to determine which of the three was to be used.

Deborah now had sufficient knowledge of phonics to be able

to sound out many words, and further phonic instruction was postponed until she felt comfortable with the knowledge she had. It was not until the instructor felt certain that Deborah was ready for more complex material that he introduced her to the more complicated vowel sounds. She was then taught the long and short sounds of the double *o* as found in "boot" and "book." He then went on to the vowels followed by *u* and *w,* which were taught to Deborah in pairs. The *ou* and *ow* were first taught and at this time the *oi* and *oy* sounds were introduced. It was explained to Deborah that these latter sounds were called diphthongs, because they were a blend of two vowel sounds and to prove it, the instructor showed that in order to say the *ou* sound as it appeared in the word "mouse" and the *oi* sound as it appeared in the word "boil," it was necessary that he change the position of his lips. The *au, aw* and the *eu, ew* sounds were then taught her, and many additional exercises that required Deborah to write on the blackboard were then performed.

While the phonic training was going on, visual training exercises aimed at increasing Deborah's visual accuracy and speed were being conducted with the tachistoscope. When a phonic principle was being introduced and learned on the blackboard, it was immediately identified in the words flashed during tachistoscopic drill. This reinforcement of Deborah's phonic lessons helped establish for her a firm grasp of phonic elements. When she read from the printed page, she was again asked to identify and sound out the vowel elements encountered. The consistency and logic of the instruction soon enabled her to sound out a number of words. Equally helpful was the fact that by sounding out words, Deborah had to examine them closely, and this helped her to retain the image of the words sounded out and enabled her to build a sight vocabulary.

It was not until Deborah was reading with some fluency that eye-movement training was initiated. Having now the basic tools and greater confidence in her ability to tackle any reading challenge, she made rapid progress and her speed began to build. Along with increased speed and fluency came better comprehension skills, and she began to look forward to a brief comprehension exercise which required that she read a short selection and answer numerous questions on its content. Deborah had gradually and in logical sequence acquired the tools necessary for developing into a competent reader.

Progress Achieved

After a total of fifty hours of daily training throughout the summer, Deborah tested out at grade level on a standardized reading test. The score she earned was grade 4.8. The achievement of average reading skills provided her with a focal point for making a successful adjustment in other areas. Although a great many problems still existed for her, her mother reported that she seemed on the way to becoming a happy child. On a number of occasions, her mother had discovered her alone in her bedroom, reading a book. She had started visiting the library once a week. And although she tended to bring home books well below her grade level, not yet having achieved sufficient confidence to tackle difficult reading material, her parents were encouraged and believed that she would soon be able to enjoy books written for her age.

Section B—Physiological Bases to Reading Problems

A FAR greater proportion of students with reading problems suffer from some physiological difficulties than is generally suspected. Physiological obstacles usually give rise in time to emotional upsets which further complicate the reading disability. If, however, the physiological obstacle can be identified early enough, specific training can often help the student to overcome the obstacle and become an effective reader. In the case of children who are young enough so that the lack of academic skills achieved has not seriously impaired their confidence in their ability to develop reading skills, training can often be particularly effective. But when a child has been struggling for a number of years with inadequate skills, he is frequently emotionally and psychologically incapable of making headway against the complex array of problems that he faces. It is therefore desirable that accurate diagnosis of any physiological obstacles to reading be made as early as possible, so that training can be provided before severe emotional factors enter the picture. To see a fifteen-year-old whose basic intelligence is high but who has lost faith in his ability to perform academic tasks is a saddening experience. When such a student is suffering from a minor deficiency which might have been diagnosed and overcome at an early age, the tragedy is all the greater.

Among the more common physiological sources of reading difficulty are mixed dominance (this category covers a very broad range of cases, all the way from a minor difficulty to a problem severe enough to make the gaining of reading skills almost impossible); faulty vision (lack of binocular vision is most commonly related to reading difficulty); faulty auditory discrimination (sometimes stemming from hearing loss); and brain damage (the degree of severity again varies over a broad range from a mild disability to a severe damage which interferes with motor as well as communication functions).

The case histories which follow were selected to provide examples of commonly encountered physical obstacles to effective reading. The purpose underlying the detailing of these cases is to provide parents and teachers with a basis for recognizing similar difficulties when encountered by them. It should be stressed that where the presence of severe obstacles is suspected, the help of a neuropsychiatrist should be sought.

Case Study 4

Student: Henry E.

Age: 9

School Grade: 2 (End of Grade 2)

Initial Reading Score: Gr. 1.5

Hours of Instruction: 40

Diagnosis

Henry's ability to concentrate on his test was limited. His mind wandered and he seemed unable to pay attention to more than one question without looking around the room for distractions. His knowledge of phonics was nonexistent except for about two-thirds of the consonants in the alphabet. He knew the names of these letters but ascribed the sounds to them uncertainly, frequently assigning the wrong sound to a letter. He did not know the names of the vowels, much less their sounds. His sight vocabulary was very small. He was able to recognize about thirty or forty words, but these, too, he frequently confused. A reversal tendency, which should have been cleared up at least two years before, persisted, and he read "was" as "saw" and "say" as "yes." His perceptual problems included leaving letters or short syllables out of words or putting them in where they did not exist. His entire reading attack was painfully slow. He stared at a word as though it might hold familiar clues, but lacking word-attack skills, he was unable to make any sense of printed material. He had been encouraged in school to skip words he did not know, but something in his nature made him reluctant to do so. The result was that he dawdled, but to no effect.

Much of the diagnostic test was administered to him orally. Simple words were spoken and he was asked to identify the initial sounds. In only a few cases was he able to do so correctly. He was a quiet boy who felt deeply his inability to make progress in reading. During the test, he evidenced his sensitivity by refusing to attempt to answer questions that were beyond him. When this occurred, his eyes would fill with tears, and he would not accept reassurance easily. On a tachistoscopic test, he showed a serious handicap when it came to identifying the symbols flashed. The reversal tendency here was strongly in evidence. If he perceived two letters, he would not only reverse the order of the letters but would frequently write the letters themselves backwards too.

A simple story was read aloud to Henry and he was then asked questions about the characters and the action. His grasp of the story was excellent, and he remembered the most detailed information with accuracy. He was then asked to do an arithmetic computation section of a nationally standardized achievement test. He performed effectively, scoring close to grade level. The confusion and difficulty that attended his work with letters and words was not apparent when he was dealing with simple arithmetic involving no more than two digits. However, when an arithmetic problem required the accurate transcription of more than two digits, he made frequent transpositions. He represented a serious remedial problem.

Henry was a severe mixed-lateral dominant. He was right-eyed, left-footed, and used both his right and left hands with equal facility. His physical co-ordination was good, and small muscle control, though in need of further development, was within a normal range for his age. His speech was without impediment, though his pronunciation of many words was somewhat slurred. He tended, also, to speak in spurts. His words tumbled out to punctuate periods of silence, but what he had to say was expressed coherently and understandably. The severity and variety of his mixed-dominant condition seemed to have interfered seriously with his perception and visual retention. It is probable that the same source had caused the lack of precision and hesitancy in his speech pattern.

Conference with Schoolteacher

Henry's teacher was an elderly woman who was obviously very much attached to the boy. She complained bitterly that the parents had no right to seek outside help for their son. She maintained that if the parents would cease putting pressure on him, he would come along beautifully. She said that he was simply not ready to read and that by trying to help him at home, his parents had aggravated his insecurity. When asked whether she was aware of any neurological obstacles that he might possess which could stand in the way of his developing effective reading skills, she maintained that his problem was purely emotional and stemmed from a highly competitive home environment in which the parents expected more from the child than he was able at that stage to achieve. When asked whether she felt his mental equipment was adequate for acquiring reading skills, she unhesitatingly said it was and that his IQ tests showed him to possess intelligence well above the average. She admitted that he did not participate in class activities as much as she would like but said this was probably again because he was not yet ready. She was asked whether his disinclination to engage in class activities might not stem from his inability to understand much of what was going on. She said simply that she was confident that he understood—he was a shy boy and she did not feel that it was wise to push him in any way. She was asked whether she had attempted to teach Henry word-attack skills through a phonic system. She said that she did not believe phonics were useful until third- or fourth-grade level when some incidental phonic instruction might help with spelling. She believed that once Henry had been exposed to reading vocabulary exercises a sufficient number of times, he would begin to remember the appearance of the words he encountered. It was pointed out to her that he had been exposed to these exercises for over two years and that his visual recall had scarcely developed. To this she replied that that only proved he was not ready to learn to read.

Conference with Parents

Henry's mother and father attended the conference together. They were deeply worried about Henry's reading problem. They had both come from a metropolitan center in the Midwest where their schooling had been oriented toward the achievement of academic skills. In attempting to compare their own development as children to that of their son, they both found cause for concern, since they were sure that the problems he was encountering were directly related to his schooling. On the other hand, they both were somewhat reticent about criticizing the teachers Henry had worked with. They found it very difficult, however, to accept the constant reassurances that were voiced from the schools every time they inquired about Henry's progress. They asked how they could make a valid judgment. Their own observation of their son convinced them that he was in serious academic trouble. The teachers and principals of the two schools attended by Henry had been telling them for two years that there was nothing to worry about and that the boy would come along if given enough time. They wondered how much time was necessary, and Henry's mother asked whether they were to wait until he entered high school before becoming concerned about his inability to read.

The results of the diagnostic test were discussed, and the effects of his mixed-dominance problem were explained carefully. The kind of phonic and visual training that was considered desirable for him was outlined.

They were then asked about Henry's home situation. Henry's mother said he had an older sister who was extremely skillful in her verbal work. She read, wrote, and spelled at a high level and had always done extremely well in school. She was two years older than Henry. He also had a younger brother of four who naturally required a good deal of the mother's time, but both the mother and father made every attempt to spend as much time with Henry as was possible. In discussing the relationship between Henry and his sister and brother, Henry's mother mentioned that she very often felt that Henry was competing against them both, but not in an overt manner. For instance, she said Henry would leave the room if his sister began to read something aloud to the family from a newspaper. On other occasions, if his younger brother was playing on the floor with some toys and one of the parents went to the younger child to see what he was doing, Henry, who was seated nearby, would get up from his seat and get down on the floor with his brother and start playing with the toys. Henry's mother thought perhaps she was making too much of these situations, but since she was so worried, she said she had been looking for any clues that might explain some of his difficulties.

It was pointed out to her that many young children were unwilling to learn to read, since reading, as was true with many other activities, represented a sign of maturity, and with maturity went responsibility. To accept the fact that one had arrived at such a stage of responsibility was to cut oneself off from the comfort and attention that was one's due in an infantile state. It was pointed out that Henry's reluctance to learn

83

to read might well have as its source his desire to continue to receive the comfort and attention that his younger brother received. On the other hand, his unwillingness to become independent of his parents (and therefore not entitled to their close attention) might well be heightened by his feeling that he could not achieve independence from them as successfully as his older sister.

Henry's mother said she believed there definitely was such an unwillingness in Henry's case, but she wondered whether putting pressure on him to improve his reading would not have unhappy side effects. She was told that this was obviously a danger but that it was believed that if Henry could be given the tools which would enable him to read on his own, a good many of his frustrations would disappear, and he would eventually gain sufficient confidence to enable him to accept his responsibilities. Before these tools could be developed by him, however, it was felt that he would have to overcome the basic obstacles to the development of reading skills which plagued him.

Conference with Student

Henry was shy and spoke little. He was asked whether or not he felt it was important for him to learn to read, and he said he wanted to read. He was told that reading was something he was capable of doing, but he would have to work hard at it. He said he knew it would be hard. It was then explained to him that the main reason he was having difficulty with his reading was that he had not learned to remember the letters and words he saw and that he would be taught how to see words so that he would remember them. He was told that this was not a very difficult thing to learn but that it was essential to learn in order to give him the ability to work with words and sentences on his own. He was assured that once he could figure out a word from its sounds, he would be able to practice by himself, and with practice, he could become a good reader.

Henry seemed highly encouraged by this conversation. He had obviously begun to feel that he was a hopeless case, and to be told that reading was within his grasp gave him great hope. It was apparent in Henry's case, as it is in almost all similar ones, that no matter how much the parents worried about his reading problems, the child worried even more.

Recommendations

Intensive visual training aimed at establishing directional habits of seeing, as well as accurate visual performance, was required. Henry would also be given phonic instruction. Along with phonic training, close work with Henry aimed at teaching auditory discrimination would be provided. He would have to learn to identify individual sounds contained within words before he could be expected to develop a phonic attack. Once visual skills and word-attack skills had been established, emphasis and training was to be shifted to achieving reading fluency, which would improve comprehension skills and extend his reading vocabulary.

Instruction Provided

Very intensive visual training was given Henry at the start. Tachistoscopic work with both nonverbal and verbal material was provided daily for fifteen minutes at a time. The verbal exercises flashed included many words which were then incorporated into phonic exercises. The phonic instruction was done on the blackboard. After Henry had been taught to listen for the sounds of letters, he was then asked to write the letters on the blackboard when the sounds were spoken by the instructor. It was necessary in the beginning that all of the consonant sounds be established in Henry's mind. This required constant drill and identification of letters in different contexts. When he had become reasonably sure of the consonant sounds, Henry worked with consonant blends and then with the consonant digraphs. It was not until these elements had been mastered that work on the vowel sounds could be attempted. Throughout this training, Henry was required to write the letters, sounding them at every step. The practice in identifying the sound, writing the letter, and sounding it, brought into play all of Henry's faculties and helped him to establish both the auditory and visual discrimination that he needed.

Once the vowel sounds were embarked on, Henry had the tools for sounding out simple words. In his case, however, the application of this phonic knowledge represented a difficult step. Children who have been instructed in a sight system and who may not have developed the ability to read still tend to model their attack on words after the sight method taught them. As a result, careful left-to-right analysis of words is foreign to them. It is frequently found that although such students may learn all of the basic phonic principles needed to make them into good readers, the application of these principles represents for them an almost impossible step, and in Henry's case, having the phonic knowledge and using it were two different things. In order to dramatize for Henry the usefulness of his understanding the sounds that were related to the letters of the alphabet, the instructor was asked to employ nonsense syllables which could be sounded phonetically. The purpose of this was to demonstrate to Henry that any sounds could be spelled, whether these sounds were words or not. Once he had learned how to sound out nonverbal sounds, he was then shown that there were a number of ways of spelling sounds that were recognizable as words. The danger in this teaching activity lies in the fact that the student may become impressed with the phonic spelling of words, which may be markedly different from the orthodox spelling. Whenever this technique is used, it is therefore necessary that the correct spelling of any word always be written for comparison with the purely phonic spelling. For instance, when Henry was asked to identify the word "gnoaz," the properly spelled "nose" was emphasized after he had identified the phonically spelled version. Likewise, "tawk," once identified, was listed as "talk." It was found that Henry began to respond to this approach, and after some initial struggle, he made the connection between letters and sounds and learned to put the sounds together to form words. The first time Henry sounded out a phonically spelled word and recognized the sounds he was putting together as a word, was for him a moment of triumph, and he derived great encouragement from this experience. His face lit up as he realized for the first time the logic underlying a phonic word attack, and he began to believe he could become a reader.

Once the basic word-recognition skills had been established, the emphasis of the training was shifted to the development of fluency. Directional progression was strengthened through the use of an eye-movement accelerator. Initially, the device was operated at very slow speeds, and the reading material used was of the simplest sort. Normal-timed reading exercises supplemented this training with the aim of helping Henry develop the ability to understand what he read. All training activities included extension of vocabulary skills. Since Henry's speaking vocabulary was above average, acquiring a phonic attack automatically provided him with a bridge between his reading and speaking vocabularies, and his reading vocabulary grew rapidly. As a result of the visual training and phonic training, he began to achieve a basic reading skill, but he still lacked confidence in his ability to handle verbal tasks, and in a test situation he tended to revert to the diffidence which had marked his attempts at academic performance from the beginning.

Reports from his school indicated that Henry was not making use of his new reading knowledge in the classroom. The teacher asserted that he showed no signs of having made any progress in his reading. Progress tests administered at the clinic showed him to be reading at the same level as when he first started training, although his daily clinic work gave evidence of real accomplishment.

Henry's parents were asked to withdraw Henry from the clinic at this time. It was explained to them that he possessed reading ability but that he would not make use of it until he felt more sure of his strength. It was believed that Henry would not use his new reading knowledge until he had proved to himself that it was really his. Until this time, he would not lay himself open to criticism by attempting reading activities, the successful performance of which was still, to him, doubtful.

Progress Achieved

Henry attended the clinic for a total of forty hours. The test he took at the conclusion of training showed him to have gained about four months in reading level. He earned a score of Grade 1.9. Five months later Henry's parents were asked to bring him in for retesting, since it was felt that his training should have been assimilated by him and would now be affecting his performance measurably. When Henry took this test, he exhibited some of the same tenseness and nervousness that always assailed him when he was being tested, but rather than being frozen into inaction, he was able to work through the test at a comparatively steady pace. By this time, Henry was midway through the third grade. He tested out just one month below grade level. His score on this test was Grade 3.3.

Case Study 5

Student: **Diane N.**

Age: **9**

School Grade: **3 (End of Grade 3)**

Initial Reading Score: **Gr. 1.4**

Hours of Instruction: **60**

Diagnosis

Diane was a nonreader. She had completed the third grade but had absorbed very little of the instruction she had received. The diagnostic reading test showed scattered and inconsistent reading habits. She was able to recognize an occasional word, but it was usually a word with which she had some specific associations rather than a word which one would expect to discover in her reading vocabulary. She had no phonic attack; in fact, Diane was unable to identify most of the letters in the alphabet and was not able to assign any sounds to the letters which she did know. Diane was a bright-eyed, hyperactive child. To sit still for more than thirty seconds required great effort on her part. She glanced over the test material quickly, making wild stabs at words which seemed to have some element of familiarity to her. Diane suffered from a severe reading deficiency.

Diane's physical co-ordination was good and she tested out

as a unilateral dominant. She was right-handed, right-eyed, and right-footed. There was no observable physiological reason for her inability to learn to read.

Conference with Schoolteacher

Diane's teacher said that she had worked intensively with Diane throughout the second and third grades. She reported that the child seemed able to grasp basic knowledge required to develop her ability to read but was unable to retain this knowledge for more than a few minutes. The teacher said that the parents had recently become very much concerned, and on the recommendation of the school psychologist, they had made arrangements for Diane to be examined by a neuropsychiatrist. Diane's teacher felt that the problem was beyond her powers. Diane, she said, was a loving and affectionate child. The teacher, however, had been disturbed by the fact that Diane had shown no concern about her inability to learn to read and did not allow the fact to interfere with her good nature and her playfulness. The teacher found that in all things not connected with academic achievement, Diane seemed to have normal intelligence. She got on well with her schoolmates and was extremely popular with them. She talked a great deal with her friends and seemed to discuss matters relevant to her age level.

Conference with Parent

When Diane's mother came to a remedial-reading clinic to discuss her daughter's inability to read, she was more puzzled than worried. She said that she and Diane's father had decided that they should get to the bottom of the difficulty and had, therefore, as a first step, taken Diane to Dr. V., a neuropsychiatrist connected with a nearby university hospital. Dr. V. was in the process of testing Diane. At the reading clinic, Diane's mother was told that no clinic training would be provided until the results of these tests were known, and she was also told that Dr. V. would be consulted and a training program worked out in conjunction with him. She was asked whether Diane had suffered any major illnesses which might have interfered with her normal development. The answer was negative. Did Diane's performance of any activities at home indicate a nervous handicap? Except for the fact that Diane was high-strung and seemed always to be on the go, neither she nor Diane's father had noticed anything which had alarmed them.

Conference with Neuropsychiatrist

A telephone conference with Diane's doctor did not throw much additional light on her problem. Dr. V. said that an electroencephalogram had been taken but had provided no evidence of brain damage. From his tests, he had concluded that although Diane's basic intelligence was within the normal range, some degree of brain damage probably existed, although he could not assert that any conclusive information had been provided by the tests. Dr. V. said that the hyperactivity and inability to retain any kind of verbal knowledge were possible symptoms of pressure on the brain. Ordinarily, such symptoms were accompanied by some disturbance of the motor system, but such a disturbance was not obvious in Diane's case. He spoke of a hydrocephalic boy, aged ten, whose academic development had been impaired. The physiological condition had cleared up of its own accord within two years of its inception, but the brain had been damaged. The damage had caused a slight limp and heaviness of physical movement, and the child's ability to perform academically had been seriously impaired. But he said that with intensive training, consisting of a great deal of repetition, the child had learned to read, though

91

haltingly. Dr. V. pointed out that whatever damage might exist in Diane's case, though probably milder from a physiological point of view than that of the case mentioned, might still be interfering deeply with her ability to grasp and retain verbal concepts. He said one of the puzzling aspects of this sort of case was the fact that such children frequently developed a perfectly normal level of skills in most activities, including in some instances, work with numbers. But the ability of these youngsters to achieve skills involving verbal concepts seemed to be particularly limited. He said that Diane had developed an average level of oral-verbal abilities and that her auditory skills were not deficient either. Reading and writing, however, presented a specific obstacle, and he was doubtful that they could be overcome, although he agreed that an intensive effort should be made to help her in these areas. It was suggested that a brief but concentrated program, relying on constant repetition of basic reading knowledge, be undertaken. He felt, however, that such a program should be continued for no more than six to eight weeks, and then discontinued for about half a year when it might be resumed for another six to eight weeks.

Dr. V. asked whether cases similar to Diane's had been encountered frequently at the clinic. He was told that they were quite rare but that it was felt that their scarcity was probably the result of improper diagnosis rather than lack of incidence. Dr. V. said that according to studies by colleagues of his, there was some indication that there was a far larger proportion of youngsters suffering from reading and writing disabilities caused by brain damage than had been suspected. He referred to the work of a neuropsychiatrist of his acquaintance who had devoted herself exclusively to the question of reading and writing disabilities caused by mild to moderate brain damage. This doctor, he reported, felt that a proportion as high as 4 per cent of the population fell into this category. He characterized this figure as no more than an informed guess, but he was convinced that further research would tend to confirm rather than to refute this hypothesis.

Dr. V. asked that he be kept closely informed of the results of any work done with Diane.

Instruction Provided

Diane's initial instruction was scheduled on an individual basis. The teaching activities were changed every ten minutes, since her attention span was so limited. She worked at first with cut-out letter blocks. She was asked to identify the letters while holding them in her hand and tracing over them with her finger. She was then asked to write the letters in her notebook and to identify them by name and the sounds they made. The same letters were flashed for her on the tachistoscope, and she was asked to print them in her notebook as each letter was flashed. After ten hours of this work, an attempt was made to have Diane put some of the simpler sounds together to form words. During any instruction session, Diane seemed to be always on the verge of grasping the material covered. At the beginning of the next session, however, it was discovered that she had retained practically nothing of the previous session's work.

At the end of twenty hours of instruction, however, it was noted that Diane's knowledge of the alphabet had begun to develop. She was able to recognize two-thirds of the letters of the alphabet by name and to print these letters from dictation. Diane was now included with a group of three other youngsters for the tachistoscopic exercises. Although working in a group had the effect of enabling her to pay attention for a longer period by strengthening motivation, she also proved disruptive to any group activity. She constantly jumped up and down and shouted out whatever came into her head. Attempts to discipline her were not effective, since she seemed incapable of restraining her bubbling spirits.

By the end of thirty hours of instruction, Diane was able to sound out about twenty 3-letter words. At this point, Diane's parents were asked to withdraw her from the clinic and bring her back six months later.

Progress Achieved

Diane returned to the clinic six months after her initial training session. It was discovered that during the intervening period, she had not increased her reading knowledge perceptibly. Her second thirty-hour session was very much like the initial one. She gained a firmer grasp of the alphabet and extended her reading vocabulary by about thirty more words. The ability to sound out words remained with Diane an isolated skill that she seemed unable to apply to any new verbal challenges. After she had sounded out a word a great number of times, she would finally learn to recognize it. If she did not recognize it, she would be reminded of its identity once she started to sound it out, but it could not be said that she developed a phonic word attack on which she could rely. The basic concepts necessary to phonic analysis required the exercise of logical principles, which seemed beyond her comprehension.

Reports on Diane's progress were furnished to Dr. V. and it was decided, on his recommendation, that Diane be sent to a private school which worked exclusively with handicapped children. This school requested reports from the clinic on Diane's work and progress during the two training sessions. The reports summarized specifically the training provided Diane and the results achieved. It was suggested that continued work on a daily basis could be expected eventually to bring Diane to about a fourth-grade level in reading; but doubt was expressed that she would ever achieve reading skills beyond this stage.

Case Study 6

Student: Gladys T.

Age: 12

School Grade: 6 (End of Grade 6)

Initial Reading Score: Gr. 5.3

Hours of Instruction: 36

Diagnosis

Gladys' test showed that she was reading with very little fluency. Simply by watching her, one could see that her eyes regressed or backtracked a number of times while reading a single sentence. At the time the test was administered, eye-movement photographs were being taken by the clinic to provide additional evidence for diagnostic purposes. (The use of this photographic technique has since been discontinued. It was determined that in the vast majority of cases, the evidence gained from the photographs merely duplicated what was learned through careful analysis of standardized tests.) In Gladys' case, the eye-movement photographs showed excessive backtracking and regression habits, indicating that her eye-movement habits were inefficient and needed development. An analysis of her standardized test provided the same information.

Gladys read very slowly. While reading silently, her lips

95

moved slightly and it was possible to see from the movements of her head that she had not developed consistent left-to-right directional habits. In those sections of the test which required fluency stemming from visual skill and good eye-mind co-ordination, her scores were particularly low. Her basic knowledge of words, however, was comparatively high, indicating that she possessed inherent verbal skills which, when developed, might be of a high order. Gladys' major problem was the establishment of reading fluency. Once such fluency was hers, she could be expected to perform at a higher level.

A phonic survey revealed Gladys had a firm knowledge of phonic principles which she applied successfully when encountering unfamiliar words.

Gladys tested out as a unilateral dominant. She was right-eyed, right-handed and right-footed. However, when faced with a visual task, she tended to slant her head in an unusual manner, as though confident only of the vision of her right eye. Her physical co-ordination was good and her handwriting was neat; however, although the letters were well formed Gladys tilted her head while she wrote.

Conference with Schoolteacher

Gladys' teacher said that she was a conscientious student but had great difficulty in completing classroom assignments. She always handed her homework in on time and it was always completely and thoroughly done. But when a test or writing assignment was given in class, Gladys rarely finished her work. The teacher had Gladys classified as a plodding, careful worker. She said, however, that she did not expect Gladys to do better than C-plus work. Her intelligence tests showed her to be a bit above average despite the fact that the scores of her achievement tests were below average. The teacher was asked whether her achievement tests had been examined with a view to establishing what proportion of the tests Gladys had been able to complete, and the teacher said that as far as she knew, no such analysis had been made. She realized that Gladys was slow and that this fact probably interfered with her ability to score well on any test; but, she felt that the school's records represented a fairly accurate record of Gladys' academic capacities.

Conference with Parent

Gladys' father attended the conference. He was very tense, and very anxious about what he considered Gladys' lack of academic ability. He himself was a graduate of a leading university and was a professional man. He said he had always assumed that Gladys would go to a good college, but the difficulties presented by her academic work had him worried. He said that she would put in hours of time on the simplest assignments at home. He had discussed the problem with her teachers and with the principal of her school. He had been told in every case that his worries were premature; Gladys was only in the sixth grade and had simply not as yet established good study habits. He said he had noticed that she read as though she were trying to memorize every word, but despite this reading approach, he found that when he questioned her on what she had read, her understanding of the material was incomplete and hazy. Gladys' father was asked whether she had any trouble with her eyes. It was explained that she tilted her head and squinted when doing visual work, as though there were some visual difficulty. He said that her eyes had just been tested once again and that he took her to an ophthalmologist every six months for eye tests, which he had been doing ever since her left eye had been operated on when she was five years old. He was asked if the operation was performed to correct a wandering eye, and he replied that she had been unable to focus her left eye. The operation had been successful from a cosmetic point of view, and the ophthalmologist had worked with her on eye exercises for more than a year in order to strengthen her ability to use both eyes together.

It was pointed out to Gladys' father that her reading difficulties probably stemmed from this visual problem, and he was told that she may not have achieved complete binocular vision. (Inadequate binocular vision frequently seems to create some confusion, and the reading performance of students with this problem usually shows lack of fluency.) Gladys' father was told that before any program including visual training was embarked on, it would be necessary to have the opinion of the ophthalmologist who had worked with Gladys.

Conference with Eye Doctor

Dr. A. said he saw Gladys about twice a year for an eye examination. He had undertaken intensive orthoptic training with her for a year following surgery. The results had been partially successful, but she had not achieved consistent binocular habits. Her ability to fuse an image was limited. She tended to rely heavily on her right eye and he had been concerned that the vision in her left eye would deteriorate rapidly. He was, however, encouraged to find that this deterioration had not taken place, although the vision of the left eye had shown no improvement. It was probable, he felt, that under certain conditions, Gladys did make use of her left eye in conjunction with her right, but he had been unable to identify precisely what conditions these were. In cases of strabismus such as this, he said the development of efficient eye-movement habits for reading purposes represented a great problem. The inability of the student to fuse an image consistently, inevitably interfered with the achievement of those co-ordinational skills required for good reading. In the case of those youngsters with whom orthoptic exercises had proved effective, the achievement of reading skills seemed to offer no excessive difficulty; but, Dr. A. said that even where orthoptic training was successful, the children usually encountered greater difficulties than did children without this visual problem.

Dr. A. was also asked whether or not he perceived a connection between strabismus and mixed-lateral dominance and he said he was aware that some authorities assumed that mixed-dominance tendencies were present in youngsters who could not fuse an image, and he felt that such an assumption was probably valid. But in the case of children whose wandering eye was the nondominant eye, he felt that diagnosis of mixed dominance might be difficult. He was told that such was the case with Gladys but that her reading pattern indicated that she was encountering the same sort of obstacles as a student who tested out as a mixed dominant. Therefore, any training provided for her would be consistent with the training given to mixed-dominant children. Dr. A. felt such a course to be justified. He said that Gladys had received as much orthoptic training as she could be expected to benefit from. He believed that although tachistoscopic and eye-movement exercises could not in any way contribute to the development of binocular vision, these exercises could go a long way toward sensitizing the retina of her right eye and thereby enabling her to perceive letters and words with greater accuracy and speed. He felt that her visual co-ordination could thereby be developed and her visual capacity enlarged, but he doubted that Gladys could ever become a superior reader.

Conference with Student

Gladys was a very intelligent girl, sensitive and perceptive. She was a quiet person, but not shy. She was very much interested in her visual problem and asked a number of searching questions about the relationship between her faulty vision and her reading difficulty. She was told frankly that through conscientious work and specific visual training, it was felt that her reading ability could be brought to a satisfactory level. It was pointed out to her that although she would probably never develop the basic co-ordinational skills necessary to read with great rapidity, she could expect to read with above-average skill. She wanted to know how fast she was reading and how fast she could expect to read. It was pointed out to her that speed in itself was important only in that it provided the fluency necessary to effective understanding. On the other hand, habits of rapid reading, which involved perceiving printed material as one reads—with the eyes and mind without recourse to vocalizing or thinking the words—probably was not in her grasp. The truly rapid reader is not conscious that he is reading words. The translation of images of groups of words into ideas is a direct, almost automatic, activity. A very high degree of co-ordination is required for the achievement of this skill. In practical terms, the speed at which such direct perception of printed material occurs is a speed between 350 to 400 words per minute. Exact speed differs with the individual and the material he is reading. The point is, however, that when a reader is absorbing material above what, for him, is a critical speed, he is reading too quickly to think each word in his mind. This critical speed is often referred to as the vocalizing barrier, because it is very difficult for a student to push beyond this speed (particularly if he has been relying on the sound of the words he is reading to help him understand). However, once a student has pushed himself past the vocalizing speed, he is no longer aware of individual words. The groups of words seen by his eyes are immediately translated into ideas by his mind and there is no consciousness of the individual words themselves.

It was made clear to Gladys that the achievement of this level of reading skill required a high order of eye-mind co-ordination and that as the result of her vision problem, it was not thought likely that she would achieve this level. On the other hand, she could be expected to develop a reading speed, with practice over a period of time, of up to three hundred words per minute, and she was assured that such a speed—even though subvocalizing habits might remain (hearing words in the back of one's mind while reading)—would make possible effective academic achievement. Gladys asked how rapidly she was reading. She was told that on the test material, which was of average difficulty for her grade level, she read at approximately 120 words per minute. She was also reminded that reading rates varied widely with the difficulty of the material being read and that it was impossible to say with accuracy that a person should read at a given rate. On the other hand, material of the difficulty encountered in the diagnostic test should have been read by her at over two hundred words per minute with better understanding than she had shown before she could be said to be reading at an average rate for her grade level. A truly effective reader at her grade level would probably read material of this kind and difficulty at speeds in excess of four hundred words per minute and with excellent comprehension. By the time such a reader had completed his high school work, he would be reading easy narrative material at speeds in excess of six hundred words per minute with good understanding. Gladys said she had heard of rapid-reading courses which spoke of achieving reading speeds of more than two thousand words per minute. She was told that such claims depended upon one's definition of the word "reading." It was possible to develop extremely efficient scanning habits which would enable the reader to cover material at speeds anywhere between two- to four- or five-thousand words per minute. Some readers who were naturally capable of reaching high levels of visual performance could grasp the major concepts at these speeds by concentrating on the structure and organization of a piece of writing. Such readers often could train themselves to grasp and to retain most of the major elements contained in a selection, and perhaps it was quibbling to say that they were scanning and not reading; but, unless they possessed a rare gift, these readers practically never comprehended more than a portion of what they read. Still, for certain purposes, this kind of effective scanning technique was extremely useful.

Gladys was told that as interesting as these questions were, her own problem represented a more interesting challenge for her. Gladys said she was confident that she could improve her reading ability.

Recommendations

Since Gladys' reading difficulty stemmed almost entirely from physiological causes, intensive visual training was called for. Tachistoscopic and eye-movement acceleration drills were indicated. Practice in word analysis, aimed at making her more efficient in phonics and word structure, could extend her vocabulary skills. This would also give her another tool for establishing fluency. The phonic attack she possessed was cautious and deliberate, although accurate. She would have to learn to combine phonics and word structure for greater efficiency in identifying printed words.

Training Provided

During the initial part of Gladys' training program, she worked on the tachistoscope with nonverbal material for three 10-minute sessions of every two-hour training period. This work was supplemented by eye-movement control exercises. Initially, material of elementary level was read by her at a comfortable speed. The speeds were gradually raised, but the level of the material remained at least two years below her capacity. Only when she was reading this easy material comfortably at three hundred words per minute on the eye-movement acceleration device was more difficult material introduced. The speed, however, was not advanced. Material of ever-increasing difficulty was introduced until finally she was reading grade-level material at three hundred words per minute. For a period, this plateau was sustained, and Gladys read numerous grade-level selections at three hundred words per minute. Only after she had grown entirely comfortable with material of this difficulty at this speed was more difficult material introduced. The speed, however, was still held at three hundred words per minute. During this time, intensive structural analysis exercises—prefix, suffix, and root drills and vocabulary development—were undertaken. On the tachistoscope, at this point, verbal material was substituted for the nonverbal, and the word-analysis drills were put into practice in relation to the words and phrases encountered in tachistoscopic drill. Gradually, the speed of the acceleration device was increased to encourage more rapid recognition.

At about 350 words per minute on the eye-movement control device, Gladys seemed to reach her ceiling. The exercises were continued at that speed, but the material grew in difficulty until she was reading first-year high-school material with good understanding.

Very little attention had been paid up to this time to Gladys' normal reading habits in regular books, since it was felt that by working exclusively on machine reading techniques, she could most easily replace her inefficient eye-movement habits. But during the latter part of the training, the emphasis was switched from mechanical reading training to normal reading training. The gap between these two types of reading procedures was bridged by intensive work on an individual pacing device, the speed of which was set first at three hundred words per minute and gradually raised to 350. Normal timed-reading exercises were alternated with the paced exercises.

Practice in prereading techniques was then introduced, but no attempt was made to teach Gladys scanning methods. It was explained to her that through daily practice on her reading, she could develop firmer eye-movement habits over a period of time, and that it would be wise for her to consider the achievement of a good scanning attack in about a year-and-a-half, when her basic reading skills were firmly established.

Progress Achieved

After thirty-six hours of instruction, Gladys showed evidence of having increased her visual skills to a point where her reading capacity was enlarged. Her normal speed was a little above two hundred words per minute. Although her retention of factual information at this speed was still not very good, she showed a definite improvement, and this improvement could be expected to continue as she practiced on her own. Verbal skills showed excellent development and the increased fluency with which she read helped her establish more effective interpretative skills. Although Gladys would probably never be a superior reader, she was on the way to establishing skills which would enable her to keep up with her schoolwork without undue strain.

Case Study 7

Student: Peter F.

Age: 15

School Grade: 10 (Beginning of Grade 10)

Initial Reading Score: Gr. 6.0

Hours of Instruction: Not scheduled for instruction

Diagnosis

When Peter took his diagnostic test, he seemed highly nervous. He questioned the value of the test in a hostile manner and performed the first two sections reluctantly. It was decided that no valid test results could be obtained under these conditions, and he was invited instead to talk about his school problems. He said that his work at school was pretty bad, and he had decided that it did not matter anyway, because the things they taught there had very little relation to life. He said he did not see that being able to spell would help him hold down a job or make a living, and for that matter, since he did not intend to become an engineer, he felt that math was another frill course.

After Peter rambled on in angry terms about school, he seemed to feel somewhat relieved. He was asked if he would try to perform a simple phonic test. He agreed grudgingly to try it. His performance on this test showed a severe phonic deficiency; but more interesting than his lack of knowledge, was his handwriting, which was composed of jagged, ill-formed letters. He had erased as much as he had written, and his paper was a mass of smudge marks. Peter wrote with his left hand, but he held the paper properly, parallel with his left forearm, so that it was not necessary for him to curl his hand around in the awkward manner of many left-handed writers. Although he was able to identify certain elements in the test, there was not one word that was spelled correctly, despite the fact that many of the words were common ones which he had encountered frequently.

The two sections of the diagnostic test which Peter did complete indicated that he had raced over the material at excessive speed, without understanding anything of what he read. It was decided that further testing would have to be undertaken before a decision was made as to whether or not work at the clinic could profitably be accomplished by Peter.

Peter tested out as right-eyed, left-handed, and left-footed. It was noticed that when Peter walked, his gait was uneven and there was a suggestion of a limp with his right foot. His right hand he kept in his pocket as much as possible. During the dominance test, he was asked if he used his right hand for anything, since he wrote with his left. He said no, because his right hand had always been weak; and when he was asked if he used his right foot—for instance in kicking a ball—he said he did not enjoy sports. His attitude throughout was defensive and agitated. It was decided not to press the examination further at this time.

Conference with Parent

Peter's father attended the conference. He was asked whether Peter had been tested by a neurologist. It was explained that his performance suggested the presence of some physiological obstacles to the development of academic skills. The father said that when Peter had been six years old, he had taken him to a neuropsychiatrist for testing, but the results had been inconclusive. Their own doctor had told them when Peter was an infant that he suffered from slight cerebral palsy and that this condition had affected his right side. He had not developed much strength in his right hand or leg. At times, particularly when Peter was tired, his right hand trembled and the boy said he could not control the trembling, although the parents had noticed that in the past two years there had been an overall improvement in his physical co-ordination.

Peter's father was told that the boy seemed excessively upset emotionally about his schoolwork, and the father said he realized this was true. He said that three years previously Peter had begun analysis with a local psychiatrist. The treatment had continued for almost three years, but Peter's anxiety had not seemed to have been eased. The analyst reported that he felt he had not been able to get to the core of Peter's problem. The analyst had tested Peter frequently during the period of the analysis. He had reported to the parents that Peter's IQ was well above average but that his emotional maturity was low.

The father said that Peter's mother had experienced so much disappointment with the boy that she had washed her hands of the problem and had told the father that it was his responsibility. The father was a busy man and said that he had been surprised to find out how desperate Peter seemed at times. He said there were times when Peter criticized everything with which he came in contact. The father said Peter had developed the habit of ridiculing his school, his analyst, his friends, his parents, and in fact, everything that was even remotely connected in his mind with his difficulties.

Peter's father was told that before any work with Peter could be undertaken at the clinic, a complete series of neurological examinations would have to be undertaken. The father agreed, and arrangements were made with a neuropsychiatrist for a report of the examination to be furnished to the clinic. At the same time, complete reports of the clinic's findings were forwarded to the neuropsychiatrist.

The clinic report stated: "The testing done here at the Clinic was concerned primarily with basic reading skills: the ability to retain visual images, to employ phonic knowledge, and to interpret printed materal and retain factual detail. An attempt was also made to ascertain the degree of eye-mind co-ordinational skill achieved.

"Academic performance is inconsistent; retention of ideas is extremely low; spelling and phonic skills are at a primary level. Physical co-ordinational skills show some confusion. He tests out as a mixed dominant: right-eyed, left-handed and left-footed. However, his medical history indicates that he has suffered from cerebral palsy from birth, which affects his right side. It is possible that Peter was meant to have unilateral right dominance, but the brain damage that weakened the right side of his body forced him to become left-handed and left-footed. This situation might well contribute to Peter's difficulty in achieving verbal skills.

"Peter's repeated failure in schoolwork seems to stem in part from his inability to retain an accurate visual image, and strephosymbolia (confusion of written symbols) is apparent. By this time, Peter's scholastic difficulties, in conjunction with other problems created by his neurological and physiological deficiencies, have led to a severe emotional condition which further denies him the ability to make academic progress."

Conference with Neuropsychiatrist

A phone conference with the neuropsychiatrist to whom Peter had been referred took place soon after the clinic's report had been received by him. Dr. X said that a primary examination of Peter had been completed and he concluded that the boy suffered from a severe malfunction of the central nervous system. Initial treatment, pending completion of additional tests, would consist of tranquilizing drugs aimed at reducing anxiety. Dr. X felt that any instruction aimed at improving reading skills would be fruitless for some time to come. He had been concerned about the problem of Peter's handedness and footedness. Gross measurement of wrists, forearms, and biceps, of thighs and calves indicated greater muscular development of the left side of the body than of the right, and Dr. X had concluded that this was obviously the result of exercise of that side of the body. He felt that although Peter was probably, as indicated in the clinic report, a mixed dominant, by the age of fifteen, many of the effects of mixed dominance should have been overcome if it had not been for neurological factors contingent on as yet unidentifiable damage to the brain.

It was agreed in Peter's case that medical treatment should take precedence over any pedagogical training. The important thing, Dr. X maintained, was that teachers be taught enough about neurological problems to be able to recognize them in their students when such problems were present.

Case Study 8

Student: Robert K.

Age: 16

School Grade: 9 (Drop-out from school in beginning of Grade 9)

Initial Reading Score: Gr. 2.8

Hours of Instruction: 50

Diagnosis

Robert's test showed him to be reading below third-grade level. It was suspected from his performance that a severe mixed-dominance condition and possibly some neurological malfunction had interfered initially with the development of his reading ability. Further testing showed him to be suffering from severe mixed dominance (complete ambidextrousness).

Conference with Schoolteacher

A schoolteacher who was a friend of Robert's family came to the clinic for a conference. She explained that she had been trying to work individually with Robert for a period of a year but had been unable to make any progress with him. He had learned to recognize some words but was unable to read third grade material coherently, since his sight vocabulary was limited and he had no phonic attack. She said that Robert had left

110

high school after a few months of the ninth grade. Because of his reading disability, he had been unable to do any of the work. He had spent many sessions with the school psychologist, but no definite conclusions had been reached. By this time, Robert was so lacking in any confidence regarding academic performance that he was unwilling to take any special training. He felt that there was no hope of his ever learning to read. She said, however, that Robert and his foster mother had decided that he should at least come to the clinic to be tested and to discuss his problem. A test appointment was made. When Robert failed to appear for his first appointment, his foster mother was telephoned and a second appointment was made. He also failed to keep that commitment. There was no further attempt made to arrange for a test.

Conference with Student

Three weeks later, Robert appeared at the clinic unannounced. A lengthy conference took place, and every attempt was made to ease his anxiety. He finally began to talk about his reading difficulties. As soon as he mentioned the problems encountered in recognizing words, his speech pattern became irregular, the words pouring out in a flood that was not always intelligible. The general order of the words was frequently confused. Occasionally, important words were left out; sometimes they were tacked on the end of a sentence.

Robert was a tall, powerfully built, handsome sixteen-year-old. He seemed basically to have high intelligence, but he experienced great frustration in expressing his ideas. Once he was feeling more comfortable, he was asked to read from a second-grade reader. He read the first sentence flawlessly and fluently. At the beginning of the second sentence, he was stumped on a word and then began to get rattled. It was as though a blind had been drawn across the page. Words which should have

111

been easy for him suddenly became incomprehensible. He was encouraged to relax and to stop trying. He closed the book and said that this always happened to him. He said for some reason the words stopped making sense. He was given a ninth-grade reader and asked to identify any words which were familiar. He picked out two or three simple words. The first two he pronounced properly; in pronouncing the third one, he transposed the two final syllables.

Robert was asked if he felt he could take a brief, simple test. He said he would like to try. The test he took was a primary test intended for Grades 1 through 3. The first question he figured out quickly; the second and third gave him more trouble, but he understood them and got them right. By this time, Robert was so nervous that he was trembling. He sat back, threw the pencil on the desk, and refused to go on, saying he couldn't do it. He was encouraged to try again. It was explained to him that he had picked up far more reading knowledge than he was giving himself credit for, and that if he would learn to concentrate without being conscious of what was going on around him, he would be able to figure out the meaning of many pages. He tried again, and this time completed a few more questions before growing tense and giving up. He was again encouraged and again he tried. For an hour, he struggled with the test, alternating between despair and enforced concentration. By the time he had completed as much as he was able of the test, he was emotionally exhausted and on the verge of tears. He was told that his effort had taken great courage. He said that he wanted some air, and he was told to step outside for a walk and to return in fifteen minutes in order to discuss the results of his test. He went outside and did not come back that day.

It was believed that Robert would return within the next few days in order to discover how he had performed on his reading test.

Recommendations

Robert returned three days later and was told that his reading test had shown that many of the basic elements necessary to reading ability had been mastered by him, and this fact should be encouraging, since it proved that he had the ability to learn enough about reading to become a reader. He was also told that it was felt that some physiological obstacle existed in him which had made learning to read so great a problem. He was given a dominance test and was found to be ambidextrous. He did not write as easily with his left hand as with his right, but he formed the letters equally well with both hands. He threw a ball with either hand and kicked with either foot. When demonstrating how he shot a pistol, he said that if he held the pistol in his left hand, he aimed with his left eye, and if he held it in his right hand, he aimed with his right eye. Robert was an excellent athlete. He played baseball with a local team. He was a switch hitter and played both first and third base, playing first base as a lefty and third base as a right-handed player. He was also very active as a skindiver. He was a member of a skindiving club which fished in the ocean every weekend. Robert said that he had an advantage over other skindivers in that he could shoot his harpoon gun from either the left or the right side of his body. Robert was a strong swimmer and the previous year had saved the life of a fellow skindiver who had become entangled in his gear.

Robert's exceptional athletic prowess had helped compensate for his academic failures. Being unable to achieve status in scholastic work, he had concentrated on achieving it through physical prowess. As a result, his academic deficiencies had not led him into antisocial behavior.

Robert's foster parents were very fond of him and had helped him to develop normally. They were sympathetic to his school problems, and although they were worried, they did not exert extreme pressure on him.

Robert was told that one of the elements contributing to his reading difficulties was his severe mixed dominance. He was told that people who had one-sided dominance were able to retain accurate visual images with less difficulty than he. Such people were right-eyed, right-handed, right-eared, and right-footed; or had equally consistent dominance on the left side. In some cases, a person might be right-handed, right-footed, right-eared, but left-eyed. In such instances, some neurologists would recommend that the person wear a patch over the left eye in order to encourage the use of the right eye for sighting purposes. Such an approach could help establish one-sided, or unilateral, dominance. In many cases, this method had proved effective. The problem of the neurologist was to determine, through an extensive series of tests, which was the naturally dominant side. Where a personal history, for instance, indicated that someone was naturally left-sided as a young child, and in adolescence was still left-eyed, left-eared, and left-footed but had been forced to use his right hand for writing, eating, and other activities, switching writing and other activities to the left hand had frequently improved reading, writing, and speech performance. And in other cases in which a person seemed naturally to be left-handed but right-eyed and right-footed, changing the handedness might be indicated. However, the decision to change handedness or eyedness should never be taken lightly, but only under the guidance of a competent neurologist. In most cases, by the time a person reached adolescence, it was questionable whether attempting to change handedness or eyedness was desirable in any event, since the co-ordinational habits established, even in the face of mixed dominance, might best be worked with and brought to a more efficient level without attempting to rearrange the basic sidedness. Through drill which exercised eye-mind-and-hand co-

114

ordination, a higher level of performance could usually be achieved.

Robert showed great interest in these explanations. He was told that his was a severe case in which the problem was not so much one of mixed dominance as it was one of lack of either left or right dominance. People who fell into this category showed no real preference for right- or left-sidedness and were usually ambidextrous as well as capable of sighting with either eye effectively. An attempt should be made in such cases, Robert was told, to decide which was the more comfortable side, and every effort should be made by such a person to rely on that side consistently.

Robert seemed puzzled at this. He said that he had always tried to maintain a balance between his right side and his left side and had always felt that his ambidextrousness was an advantage to him rather than a disadvantage. He was told that although in certain sports this might be true, the reliance on both sides had probably been a factor which interfered with the development of reading and writing skills. He asked how this could be and was told that very little was known about the underlying causes. It was known, however, that for a right-sided person, the left side of the brain was dominant and for a left-sided person the right side of the brain was dominant. When there was a mixture of dominance, there was evidently some obstacle to the smooth and accurate transmission of messages from the eyes to the brain and from the brain to the hands or feet. It was this obstacle which interfered with the development of the kind of effective co-ordination which made proficient reading and writing easy.

Robert was told that in his case, since everything was almost perfectly balanced (ambidextrous), it would be sensible for him to continue using his right hand for writing, but he should attempt to perform other activities with his right hand as much as possible. In the meantime, it was hoped that left-to-right directional visual training would help him to establish a basis for developing word-recognition skills.

Conference with School Counselor

Robert had left school almost a year prior to his diagnosis at the clinic. The man who had been his counselor at school reported that the school records showed Robert to have above-average intelligence, but his final overall academic achievement was about third-grade level. The counselor said that Robert had been referred to the district psychologist when he was in the fourth grade. By that time, it had become apparent that he was not learning to read. At that time, Robert had been living with his natural parents. The psychologist's report stated that although there were emotional elements at work that made it difficult for Robert to achieve scholastic skills, the effect of these elements was not easy to determine. Robert's home life at that time was considered to be normal, although the family was labeled "underpriviliged." By the time Robert had been advanced to fifth grade, his home situation had changed radically. He had been abandoned by his parents, became a ward of the Court, and had been put into a foster home (the same one in which he was currently living). Robert had then been sent to a neurological clinic where he was tested for brain damage. The tests were negative. This background, the counselor said, had evidently satisfied the district psychologist that Robert's difficulties stemmed primarily from emotional sources. The counselor felt that there was no question but that Robert's schoolwork had suffered as a result of his rejection by his natural parents, but he said that this fact still did not explain why Robert had not learned to read during the time he was still with his own family. By the time the counselor had met Robert, the boy was entering the ninth grade, the pattern of failure had been well established, and it seemed there was little hope of reversing the situation. Robert attended classes, sat quietly, but made no effort to keep up, since he felt that the classwork was beyond his grasp. He was, however, accepted by his classmates and was popular with them.

The counselor said that the schools were frequently criticized for promoting students like Robert when it was obvious that they could not do the assigned work, but he didn't know what other course the schools could take. It was not reasonable to keep Robert in the third grade indefinitely, since he would become further disturbed himself and present a distraction to the other children. Though he had absorbed very few academic skills, he had been with children of his own age and his social and emotional development had continued, so that he was at least an acceptable member of his group socially. As long as the school had to accept the responsibility for every child, the counselor insisted, it would have to accept responsibility for the Roberts. A measure of the partial success of the school was the fact that Robert had never shown signs of excessive rebellion and had never been in trouble with the police. There was also to be considered, the counselor continued, the fact that although he was unable to perform scholastically at the level of his contemporaries, Robert had still gained both a great deal of information and the ability to think rationally simply from having been present during class discussions. On rare occasions, he had even been known to enter into these discussions. The counselor maintained that although Robert had been unable to take full advantage of his schooling, he had still not entirely wasted his time while at school.

The counselor was asked why Robert had left school during the first semester of the ninth grade. The counselor replied that by that stage, the emphasis on academic achievement had begun to make the boy self-conscious about his shortcomings. He had been offered a job as a stock boy at a local sport shop. Because he was sixteen, he was able to get work papers and was allowed to leave school. Unfortunately, the job had lasted only a few months and Robert had been trying to find other work since that time. Lacking the ability to read, however, he had been finding it almost impossible to get a job. The counselor had seen him a short time before and had also suggested to Robert that perhaps the clinic could help him to develop sufficient skill in reading to enable him to find the kind of work at which he would be happy.

The counselor was told that it was doubtful that much could be done for Robert. Although he possessed some of the basic information necessary to become a reader, the confusion in his mind with regard to these elements had created a further obstacle. But more than this, the only hope that Robert would become a reader rested on his willingness and ability to put forth a sustained and intensive effort. He was so lacking in confidence that it would be very surprising if such an effort could be made by him.

The counselor wondered if the situation might have been different had Robert been given special instruction at an early age. He was told that the chances for success would have been increased, since Robert's emotionally disturbed condition had most probably been less severe six or seven years before, but the severity of his dominance problem would always have represented a serious obstacle to his establishing reading skills. It was pointed out that the mixed dominant who seemed to lack either a left or right preference, and was therefore ambidextrous and both left- and right-eyed, generally seemed to have greater difficulty in establishing a reading pattern than did the mixed dominant who was strongly left-handed and strongly right-eyed, or right-handed and left-eyed. The counselor was told that these generalizations applied only to the most severe cases. Robert's dominance problem, however, had always been a severe one.

Conference with Parent

Robert's foster mother attended a conference shortly before Robert started training. She explained that she had always been in a difficult position where Robert was concerned. Both she and her husband were very fond of the boy and their lives revolved about him, but whenever any important decision regarding his life had to be made, they did not feel free to make it without first clearing the project with the authorities who were ultimately responsible for Robert's care. She was asked why she and her husband had not adopted Robert. She said that this was not possible. She had looked into the matter and discovered that an aunt of Robert's had been wanting to adopt him, but the welfare authorities did not feel that the aunt could provide a suitable home for the boy. On the other hand, the interest of any member of his family in him made it difficult, if not impossible, for outsiders, such as she and her husband, to gain legal custody except on a foster-parent basis.

Whether or not this version of the legal disposition of Robert's case was accurate is not known. It was obvious, however, that she wished to do everything within her limited power to help solve Robert's problem. She said that she and her husband had just bought a used car for Robert. They had not shown it to him as yet, because he had expressed worry over whether or not he would be able to get a driver's license, since he was unable to read. They knew that for him to have the car and not be able to drive it would be terribly frustrating for him. They had, therefore, decided that they would not tell him about the car until he was able to read well enough to pass his driver's test. It was pointed out to her that although there might be elements of cruelty involved, it would still be realistic to tell Robert about the car in order to equip him with additional motivation for overcoming his reading difficulties. On the other hand, she was told, if his reading did not progress as well as was hoped, he should still be able to get his license, since the Department of Motor Vehicles provided an oral test for illiterates in which the only reading required was recognition of commonly encountered road signs.

It was made clear to Robert's foster mother that any hope of his achieving effective reading skills would depend upon whether or not he would be able to make a sustained effort. She was told that Robert would inevitably encounter a series of minor failures during each session of instruction and that these small failures would be extremely discouraging, despite the fact that they would be offset by small successes. Robert had long since ceased to believe, deep within himself, that he could become a reader, and it was doubtful if the necessary confidence could be developed in him.

Instruction Provided

In the initial stages of Robert's training, it was decided that he should receive individual instruction. The first sessions were concerned with basic phonic instruction. Robert had comparatively little difficulty in identifying single syllables; however, when two syllables were put together to form a word, he would begin to grow confused. He would pronounce the second one first as often as he would pronounce the syllables in correct order. He would then grow tense and start to stammer, and within a short time, he was perspiring from anxiety. He was constantly reassured and encouraged, but each hour's work was an ordeal for him. Painfully, bit by bit, Robert began to grow more relaxed. Tachistoscopic work gave him an opportunity to succeed. Although he transposed the images flashed, his perception of them began to grow in accuracy with practice, but his progress was extremely slow.

After twelve hours of work, he mentioned offhandedly that his parents had given him a car and that he wanted to learn to read the instruction manual, which would prepare him for taking the test for his driver's license. He had the manual in his pocket, and words were selected from it and then sounded out by him. For the next ten hours of instruction, all blackboard exercises were drawn from words encountered in the *Motor Vehicle Code*. Robert got to the point where he was thoroughly familiar with the words appearing on road signs. Of course, the shape of the signs provided him with an additional clue as to what word appeared on the sign, but even when the words were written on the board, he was soon able to recognize them. When he was stuck, he would start sounding out the initial syllables of the word, and that reminded him of the word he was deciphering.

One day Robert arrived with the *Motor Vehicle Code* in his hand and read an entire paragraph fluently, without stopping. He then laughed, self-consciously. When asked whether he had sounded out the words in the passage, he confessed that his foster mother had read the paragraph to him. He was asked how many times she had read it, and surprisingly, he said that she had read it only once.

Robert was asked if he always remembered things that he heard only once, and he said that if he were interested in something and could find someone to read it to him, he usually could remember it accurately. Robert was told that this was a valuable skill and that he had developed it as a substitute for reading. He said that his teachers at school seemed to think that he did not know what was going on in class, but he usually understood what they were talking about, as long as the material had been covered by the teacher's lecture or in a class discussion. He did not forget things that he had heard. It was only when schoolwork involved reading assignments that he had been lost.

Robert was told that this exceptional retention of what he heard was very common among people who were poor readers.

It was pointed out to him that this skill would be a real advantage to him once he was able also to read well and to retain the information he gained from books and magazines.

Robert was tested at this point in order to determine specifically what progress he had made. Taking a primary level test was not as nerve-racking an experience for him as it had been the first time, but it still was a painful process. On this test, Robert performed at a grade level of 4.7. He was very much encouraged by the results, and for the next ten hours of instruction, applied himself conscientiously. He read very haltingly, having to sound out each word, and by the time he had completed a paragraph, he was exhausted by the effort.

During this period, he went to the Motor Vehicle Bureau, was given an oral test, and earned his driver's license. Within a few weeks after he had been driving his car, he began to skip instruction sessions. He was phoned and told that although he still had a long way to go, he had made real progress, and it would be a shame if he gave up his instruction at that time. He resumed regular attendance and was now put into a small group comprised of three other youngsters who were a year or two his junior and who were themselves having serious difficulties. Robert worked well with these children, but rather than being further motivated by group work, as had been hoped, he found the competition discouraging. He withdrew into himself after discovering that his fellow students performed certain learning tasks more easily than he. Robert was taken out of this group and individual instruction was resumed.

At the end of forty-two hours, another test was administered. Robert struggled with the test, reverting to his previous confusion. He tested out at Grade 4.1. During a conference held with him at the conclusion of this test, he was told that he could not expect his progress to be consistent but that with steady application he would eventually achieve greater fluency. The learning curve is an irregular one, comprised of periods of rapid growth as well as periods of no evident progress. When a student reaches a certain plateau, it takes courage to persist, even though he does not seem to move ahead; but a breakthrough usually takes place when least expected and the student finds himself on a higher plateau. When this explanation was finished, Robert began to shake his head. He said that he could not do it any more. He was all mixed up, and every time he saw a book, he wanted to throw it out the window. He said that he did not care if he ever saw a book again. He did not care if he ever learned to read. He was trembling and his face was white. He was told that perhaps he was right; perhaps it would be wise for him to discontinue instruction for about a month or two.

About nine weeks later, Robert appeared at the clinic and said he wanted to do some more work. He had found a job driving a delivery truck for a local grocer. He said he had been thinking that if he could learn to read well enough, he would like to go back to high school and get his diploma.

Robert resumed instruction shortly thereafter. At the beginning of the first session, he seemed more relaxed than he had been previously, but by the end of the training period, he was once again tense and anxious. He attempted six more hours of instruction but seemed to make little or no progress. He continued to stumble over words he had seen hundreds of times and still transposed syllables and letters. He announced that he was not getting anywhere. Robert did not return for any additional instruction.

Progress Achieved

Robert had received a total of about fifty hours of instruction. On the timed tests, he was able to read at approximately fourth-grade level, but very haltingly. It seemed probable that Robert would have difficulty learning to read much beyond this level. The combination of physiological and emotional problems which had beset him made additional achievement unlikely. In a terminal report to Robert's foster parents, they were urged, as they had been two or three times during Robert's training period, to have Robert examined by a neuropsychiatrist; however, they were cautioned not to expect that any additional light might be thrown on his condition. The pattern of his reading performance was not consistent with that of a person who had what is called "word blindness" (alexia). Robert saw and recognized the elements of words but seemed confused by the directional aspects of reading. Word blindness was usually connected with some sort of brain damage, and from Robert's overall performance, as well as the tests that had been performed on him years before, it was doubted that any identifiable damage had been sustained.

The only question remaining was whether or not, if Robert had undergone intensive reading training at the primary level, his difficulties might have been overcome. It was felt that in all probability, more substantial progress would have been made at an earlier age, since Robert's reading problem would not have been so greatly complicated by emotional factors.

Case Study 9

Student: John C.

Age: 20

School Grade: 15 (Beginning of College Junior year)

Initial Reading Score: Gr. 6.0 (Approx.)

Hours of Instruction: 30

Diagnosis

John's ability to take a diagnostic reading test was seriously impaired, as was his ability to take any test, by the fact that he read without fluency. John was able to complete a very small portion of any section of the test. Those questions which he did complete were answered with only a fair degree of accuracy. The only area in which he displayed any promise was in the vocabulary section of the test concerned with words encountered in isolation rather than in context. The general picture of his test results indicated a lack of any consistent eye-movement pattern and an inability to derive any coherent sense from written material. The diagnostic phonics survey showed a serious deficiency in phonic knowledge. However, there was some evidence in his performance on this test of an understanding of basic phonic principles, although this understanding was too unspecific to provide him with a useful verbal tool. John had obviously been able to figure out certain elements of phonics on his own, but this knowledge was disorganized and limited.

John tested out as left-eyed and right-handed. Footedness was also right-sided. He wrote haltingly when faced with words which were not extremely familiar to him, hesitating over the order in which the letters were to appear, but there were no reversals in the completed writing. On the other hand, the hesitation was marked by half-completed letters, which were then written over, and by frequent erasures. Close observation of John, however, revealed good physical co-ordination. He moved gracefully and confidently; he spoke easily and without the hesitation that marked his writing. A tachistoscopic test on nonverbal material revealed, however, a marked inability to retain an accurate visual image of more than two or three digits.

Report from College

John's grades averaged about C-minus. The courses requiring a great deal of reading, such as History and English, were barely at the passing level. However, his grades in mathematics and physics were C-pluses and B's. His reasoning ability was obviously at a high level, but his academic skills were so faulty as to present an obstacle to effective performance.

Conference with Parent

John's mother was an elementary schoolteacher. She was highly intelligent and well versed in the entire area of reading problems, but she felt that John's difficulties were too complex to be susceptible to the sort of training she was able to offer. She reported that John's intelligence tests throughout his school life had shown him consistently to possess superior intelligence, but his achievement tests had consistently revealed deficiencies in verbal capacity. John had always been a co-operative and helpful child, she reported, and there had always been a close and happy relationship between he and his parents. He was a very conscientious worker and worried deeply about his schoolwork. The heavy demands made on him by his college assignments had made him even more tense than previously about his reading problems, and he was very anxious to overcome these difficulties. He had supplied himself with numerous self-help books on reading and had worked assiduously with them, but to small effect. As a result, he was discouraged and diffident about the prospects of his ever becoming a facile reader and an efficient student. She reported that John had always lacked confidence in an academic situation, but that since he had been in college, he had become more silent and withdrawn than before. He was generally unhappy with himself and had threatened frequently to leave school, despite the fact that completing his college work was very important to him.

Conference with Student

On the surface, John was poised and pleasant. He was, however, very seriously concerned about his reading. He spoke about the difficulties he encountered in trying to prepare his school assignments. It took him many hours to complete the simplest academic task. He had to go over a paragraph numerous times before the sense of it came to him, and he was always in fear that the following day his recollection of any material would be inadequate. He was very conscious of the ease with which many of his friends at college were able to do their schoolwork and seemed convinced that they were far more intelligent than he, except in mathematics. He reported that he would often offer to help his associates with their mathematics or physics assignments and that he spent a good deal of time in this way; he knew that the time should have been spent on his own English and History assignments.

John was upset as much by his spelling difficulties as by his poor reading. He complained that writing a report or paper took him forever, since he had to look up every other word in a dictionary. Also, although he knew which word he would want to put on paper, he would have only the vaguest idea of what letters to use while writing it.

He had never heard anything about mixed-dominance difficulties but said he had often wondered why he found shooting a rifle an awkward activity. In demonstrating how he held and aimed a rifle, he extended his left arm as a right-handed person would, but sighted with his left eye. He said he was not a good shot.

John was anxious to undertake any training that held out the possibility of his overcoming his reading problems.

Recommendations

The initial aim of any training provided for John was to help establish left-to-right directional habits. In the event the training offered at the clinic did not prove effective within a short time, it was suggested that John be referred to a neurologist for examination. However, inasmuch as his physical co-ordination was good, it seemed doubtful that such a course would be necessary.

The emphasis of a reading training program would lie in the area of developing visual skills. Tachistoscopic work and eye-movement control exercises would be undertaken intensively. At the same time, instruction in phonics and word structure could be expected to strengthen his word-identification skills. Specifically, through intensive phonic training, it was hoped that the directional aspect of reading and writing would become second nature and the hesitations about the order in which letters appeared in a word would be overcome. The combination of visual and phonic training could be expected to develop habits of visual retention along with a more effective eye-movement pattern. Efficient co-ordination between eyes and mind would, it was hoped, be developed.

Instruction Provided

In accordance with the program discussed above, John undertook intensive daily work at the clinic. He attended two hours a day, five days a week. After twelve hours of training, most of which was concentrated on visual and phonic skills, progress was recorded in achievement of greater visual accuracy, extended eye span, and more rapid perception of visual images. Exercises in word structure included prefix, suffix, and root drill. Vocabulary drills were supplemented by intensive home study, which John performed conscientiously. He also practiced timed reading exercises daily at home. Although spelling skills showed small improvement during this early phase, some evidence of a systematic word attack began to be evident. John automatically stopped skipping unfamiliar words; he no longer looked solely for context clues to help him decipher a passage; he strove to sound out those words which were unfamiliar to him. He had been instructed to work out each word as it appeared, having been told that in this way he would more readily gain familiarity with words, since attacking them phonically provided more intimate contact with them than guessing at them from context. A recognition vocabulary would most readily be built in this way.

During the next twelve hours of instruction, the emphasis of the training was shifted to comprehension exercises co-ordinated with eye-movement acceleration drills which were aimed at increasing speed. The tachistoscopic work had helped develop John's visual capacity and co-ordinational skills; the

129

eye-movement activities continued this development. At the same time, the comprehension-question materials taught John to organize the ideas contained in a passage as he read them. The questions also reinforced in him a sense of responsibility for what he read. During this phase, John began to read many hours a day at home, constantly forcing himself to read more quickly.

Toward the latter part of this period, John was introduced to prereading and scanning techniques which further emphasized the need to identify the major concepts contained in any passage. The structure of the reading material had to be established in his mind in order for him to retain what he read.

For the first sixteen or eighteen hours of instruction, John was vocalizing as he read. Every word was spoken silently to himself. He had come, through habit, to rely on saying the words to himself in order to help himself understand what he was reading. By the end of sixteen to eighteen hours, John had reached a speed at which vocalizing was difficult (375 to 400 words per minute). At this point, he was subjected to very intensive acceleration exercises on an individual pacing device. His eye-movement habits had been sufficiently well established on the eye-movement accelerator for the vertical pacer to prove effective, and by the time twenty-four to twenty-six hours of instruction had been completed, John was reading with his eyes and not with his mouth. When he was first forced beyond a speed at which he could vocalize, his comprehension of material fell radically, but as soon as his mind adjusted to nonvocalizing speeds, comprehension began to build, and before long was stronger than it had been. With increased fluency and the additional volume of reading which it made possible, John's familiarity with words began to make itself shown in his vocabulary skills, and beginnings of progress in spelling habits became apparent.

Progress Achieved

John attended the clinic for a total of thirty hours. His reading speed increased enormously and he was better equipped to take a test with some expectation of success. His dramatic increase in test scores on his terminal test was the result, primarily, of the increased fluency with which John was reading, but through his conscientious application, the gains made in all areas of reading skills were unquestionably remarkable. John's accomplishment is, unfortunately, not always duplicated by students whose initial reading, writing, and spelling problems seem to stem from a mixed-dominance condition. Training such as provided for John, when accompanied by conscientious home study, will, in the majority of cases, produce measurable gains.

Although John C. has still further to develop verbal skills and co-ordinated reading and study habits, he has made the first long step toward this goal, and his capacity for doing college work has been enhanced. Additional concentration will be required before the skills he has achieved will be maximally useful to him scholastically, but the basic tools are now available to him.

Section C—Emotional Bases to Reading Problems

It is almost impossible to categorize the emotional difficulties which underlie reading problems, since every reading problem has its emotional components. An attempt has been made in this section to identify only some of the more obvious emotional factors which militate against the acquisition of reading skill. As has been noted above, many of these factors have, as their particular source, physiological obstacles to reading development, but many children are sufficiently upset from purely emotional causes to make it difficult for them to develop any complicated skill. Their powers of concentration and their ability to reason coherently make them no more able to become effective readers than to become mathematicians or musicians.

Students whose reading difficulties seem to stem exclusively from emotional upset seem better able to develop a high level of reading skills, and the prognosis for such students is generally more favorable than for those who also have some physiological difficulty. Of course, youngsters in this category have usually developed blocks about certain aspects of reading, but consistent instruction which is offered with encouragement and

132

understanding and contains a great many repetitive exercises can go a long way toward easing the tensions which created the blocks. The term "mental or emotional block" is in itself an unfortunate designation, since it connotes an immutable condition, and for many years, entirely too many teachers have used the term to excuse themselves for not making progress with a student. It is true that with the student-teacher ratio that exists in most of our schools, the teacher is unable to provide the intensive individual instruction which is so helpful in overcoming a youngster's emotional problems, but schools must continue to make every effort to provide the special instruction needed.

The case histories that follow provide portraits of students whose reading difficulties seemed to stem primarily from emotional sources. These cases are not intended to represent a definitive or complete study of the relationship between emotional upsets and reading deficiency, but rather to provide some indications of the sort of problems with which too many children are wrestling.

Case Study 10

Student: **Thomas J.**

Age: 9

School Grade: 3 (Beginning of Grade 3 after having been retained in Third Grade)

Initial Reading Score: **Gr. 1.6**

Hours of Instruction: 60

Diagnosis

Testing Tommy was a challenging experience. His attention
span was so short that he could not be left alone to complete
any of the test sections. He would work on a question, then
immediately run to the person who was administering the test
for reassurance. As a result, it was impossible to time the test
he took in accordance with directions. It was thought wisest,
in conformance with usual practices when testing this sort of
youngster, to allow Tommy to complete as much of the test
as he was capable of completing, without reference to the time
factor. Tommy tested out at the sixth month of first-grade level,
or approximately two and one-half years below the level at
which he would have been reading had he been an average
student. In other words, in over three years of schooling (not
including kindergarten), Tommy was reading only as well as
an average youngster who has been in first grade for a little

over one semester. His reading training had consisted of phonic instruction from the start. He had attended a parochial school from first grade, and intensive, individual attention had been given to him. Special instruction from a reading teacher provided by the school had been afforded him, and he had been drilled consistently on phonograms and word families. He had not been able, however, to develop a sight vocabulary of any size, and even the most frequently encountered words had to be sounded out by him a syllable at a time.

Tommy's spelling was, in general, consistent with the sounds of the simple words he labored with, but he made the *k* sounds always with a *k,* the long *e* always as a double *e,* and the long *a* always as *ay.* His spelling, though phonically accurate, bore little relation to correct spelling, since he was unable to remember which letters were associated with which words. Whenever a word was outside his experience, he was lost when it came to spelling it, because his auditory discrimination was as weak as his visual retention. He was unable to isolate the sounds within any given word.

The diagnostic reading test provided only very limited information on Tommy's problem; conferences held were more fruitful.

Tommy tested out as right-handed, right-footed, and left-eyed. The degree of severity of his dominance problem was difficult to gauge since other factors weighed so strongly. However, the mixed-dominance element certainly played a part in his difficulties. The fact that Tommy had been instructed in a rigid phonic system to little effect was contrary to usual experience with laterally confused youngsters, who generally respond favorably to phonic instruction. The inability to develop visual retention would, of course, militate against his learning with accuracy the phonograms necessary to build an effective phonic attack, but it was believed that the difficulty went beyond the physiological. Physical co-ordination was observed to be smooth and normal. His speech was excellent, the words well formed and the ideas coherently expressed. Handwriting was cramped and tense, and great pressure was exerted on the pencil. Each letter was formed distinctly but separately from all the other letters. One letter differed in size from its neighboring letter, although taken separately, each letter was well shaped. In writing a word, Tommy would frequently get halfway through and then abandon the task. Sufficient effort to complete any word was rarely put forth. Interruptions and distractions seemed actively to be sought by him in order to justify the incapacity to complete even brief activities.

Conference with Schoolteacher

Tommy's schoolteacher wished to be very helpful but was puzzled by his lack of achievement. She said that while talking to him, one realized that he was alert and intelligent, interested in all subjects and able to discuss them with surprising maturity, and possessed of a great deal of information. None of this oral-verbal skill was available to him, however, when it came to reading and writing. She had worked with him individually over a long period of time, but each day he seemed to have forgotten what he had learned the day before. It was as though he had erased from his mind everything that she had managed to inscribe there the previous day. He was a difficult problem in class. During discussion periods he constantly jumped to his feet and shouted out answers to questions without waiting to be called on. He tended to monopolize any discussion in which he took part. Disciplining him had only a momentary effect. Two minutes later, he would do again the very thing for which he had been punished. Receiving constant attention seemed to be an ever-present need for Tommy.

His teacher was asked about his intelligence tests, and she said he tested out badly; however, little credence was given any tests Tommy took, since he was unable to complete any questions which were posed to him. She felt, as a lay teacher, that psychological help was called for, but the school policy had always been opposed to such outside aid.

With regard to his personal life, she knew very little. His father had died when he was six, and his stepfather was extremely conscientious about the boy's upbringing. The stepfather frequently got in touch with the school with requests that special reports on the boy's problems be sent home.

The teacher was relieved to learn that Tommy's parents were seeking outside help, but she was skeptical that real progress could be made with him.

Conference with Parents

Both Tommy's mother and stepfather attended the initial conference. The stepfather did most of the talking, asking many questions to which answers were not available. He was a fairly intelligent person who seemed genuinely concerned about Tommy's difficulties. He was an orderly, somewhat careful man and had set up a schedule of study for the boy. He was vaguely distressed that Tommy had not kept to the schedule conscientiously. The mother interrupted to detail the history of Tommy's reading problem. It was a long, rambling, largely irrelevant account that covered the history of reading problems in her own family as well as in the families of neighbors. She was intent on what she had to say but had obviously been unable to reach any helpful conclusions about Tommy's shortcomings. Her husband listened to her account impatiently, as though anxious for the interruption to cease, so that he could get on with the important business of pinning down Tommy's problem and establishing a concrete regimen for overcoming it. It was pointed out that the chances of achieving any dramatic improvement in Tommy's reading were not good, although it was felt that some progress might be made through concentrating on the development of visual retention. It was strongly urged that the services of a psychologist be sought, and the names of persons competent to provide this kind of help were furnished. Both parents were reluctant to act on this suggestion, feeling that Tommy's problems were specifically related to his studies rather than to his personality. Tommy's mother said that if only the boy would settle down, everything would be all right. The stepfather said that he was an accountant and that he had encountered very few problems in his life that could not be solved once you had them in front of you on paper.

Conference with Student

Tommy talked incessantly and intelligently. For the most part, he talked about his tropical fish and how he raised them, about his parakeets and how he was teaching them to talk by separating them, and about the astronomy charts that his teacher had shown to his class in school that day. He had absorbed a remarkable amount of accurate information and talked about it creatively. His use of words was skillful and accurate. He spoke in a confidential and assured manner. When he was interested in a subject, he gave it his undivided attention, and one was able to converse with him most satisfactorily. He talked about school freely and without reservation, as though he enjoyed every moment he spent there. He talked with respect and interest of the things his teacher had told him as well as of things his parents had brought home for him or talked to him about. Nowhere was there any indication of tension or dissatisfaction. He ignored his reading problems completely. When asked why he felt he was having such difficulty in learning to read, he pondered for a moment and replied that he felt he was doing better, after which he immediately launched into a discussion of guppies and water temperature.

Recommendations

It was felt that the hope of achieving any substantial gains with Tommy were small as long as the efforts were restricted to the area of providing reading training alone. Although it was believed that extensive visual-training experience, coupled with word-recognition instruction emphasizing phonics, might serve to give him a start toward building a bridge between his speaking and his reading vocabulary, Tommy's instructor was asked to prepare detailed weekly reports for submission to the parents and to the school in the hope that they would recognize the need for a broader and more profound attack on Tommy's difficulties.

Inasmuch as Tommy was compensating for his reading and writing difficulties by having developed exceptionally high auditory and oral skills, the need for intensive silent-reading activities was indicated. Blackboard work, with emphasis on kinaesthetic participation by Tommy, was to be undertaken daily. His phonics training would be coupled with auditory-discrimination exercises. When writing on the blackboard, Tommy would be asked to identify the sounds of the letters he wrote. The parents were asked to use Tommy's interest in tropical fish and birds to advantage. They were asked to find library books for him at first-grade level on these subjects and to encourage him to further his knowledge in these fields, not by talking, but by reading.

Instruction Provided

Tommy's instructor worked intensively with him to relate phonic knowledge to visual images. Tommy was prohibited from discussing the irrelevant matters that were always uppermost in his mind, and he was gently reminded constantly that he had to apply himself to the task at hand. His tendency to take over any discussion and steer it into channels with which

139

he was conversant was discouraged from the start, and he was assigned brief and specific reading and writing exercises which were closely and continuously checked.

Tommy's ability to concentrate on relevant activities improved for a time, but the moment the demands of his work began to be challenging, he resorted to every conceivable means of avoiding performance. At first he tried disappearing to the restroom whenever he felt the instructor was ready to check his work. When he had been discouraged from this tactic, he went further by locking himself in the restroom and not responding when the instructor attempted to find him. Numerous talks with the boy aimed at reassuring him about his ability to achieve reading skills seemed to have only a very temporary effect.

Tommy began to bring articles to his instructor with the purpose of providing a basis for conversation which would preclude his getting down to work. He brought into play a number of clever techniques for striking up conversations with any adults who might be present. He seemed compulsively unwilling to tackle his reading and writing activities and employed desperate means for avoiding assigned work.

Tommy's instructor felt that perhaps another man might get better results, and Tommy was reassigned to a different instructor. For a time, he applied himself, and some further increase in his ability to retain visual images was noted, but eventually the same pattern of distracting activities began to appear.

Whenever any member of the staff spoke to Tommy in an effort to engage his interest, he responded enthusiastically, and it was felt that progress was being made; however, the moment the time came for him to read or write, his interest disappeared.

It was suggested that the special instruction at the clinic be interrupted in the belief that the intensive pressure on him was beginning to bore the boy. He was removed from the clinic for a few weeks, and when he returned, it was found that he worked well for a short time, and then relapsed into the previous pattern.

All this time, reports indicating the need for more thorough-going analysis and training were being sent both to Tommy's parents and to his school. Finally, another conference was held with both parents (Tommy's stepfather had appeared about once a week to discuss the boy's problems throughout the training provided). At this final conference, the gains made by Tommy were pointed out and the parents were told that unless they were willing to arrange for the boy to receive psychotherapy, no further work could be done with him at the clinic. At this point, Tommy was withdrawn.

Progress Achieved

Tommy attended the clinic for a total of sixty hours over a six-months' period. His total gains during that time amounted to a six-months' increase in reading level. The score he earned on his terminal test was Grade 2.3. His sight vocabulary had increased, but he had not developed workable word-identification skills. His general attitude toward reading had not changed appreciably, and his previous problems had not been overcome.

Tommy's schoolteacher reported no noticeable change in his behavior in class. She had recommended to the school that he be removed from her class. The school told her that if she would not work with him, he would have to be taken out of the school. She felt that she was not getting any results with him and was afraid that he would have to leave and attend some other school.

Tommy's problem called for more than intensive reading instruction. Accurate diagnosis of his difficulties, both psychological and neurological, should have been made before a specific course of action involving reading abilities alone was attempted.

Case Study 11

Student: Edward L.

Age: 15

School Grade: 10 (Middle of Grade 10)

Initial Reading Score: Gr. 4.0 (approximately)

Hours of Instruction: 14

Diagnosis

Edward took the diagnostic reading test unwillingly; and then, only to satisfy his suspicions as to the purpose of the test. He came to the clinic the first time to look over the place and to chat with the people working there. His manner was breezy, and on the surface, poised. The only evidence of anxiety was the extreme vigor with which he chewed gum. His second visit to the clinic was unannounced; he dropped in casually one afternoon and talked constantly about a play-reading that he wanted to participate in at school. He mentioned offhandedly that he had to find someone to read the play to him, so that he could familiarize himself with the words. This was his only reference to his reading difficulties. Edward's third visit to the clinic found him ready to be tested. He took the test in what appeared to be an expert manner. He gave every appearance of being perfectly familiar with the material and seemed to experience no difficulties. He did not once frown at a question.

142

He seemed to apply himself to the test, but without any hint in his manner to indicate that he might be under any pressure. He gave an excellent imitation of a proficient, capable student. The test results indicated a severe reading deficiency—Edward had evidently been able to read practically nothing of the test. He had no phonic attack and had to rely on his ability to recognize the few words which were familiar to him. The only area of the test in which he showed any degree of ability was the study-skills portion. This required finding sentences in the text which answered specific questions. In a sense, this exercise required the student to match up words in the text with words in the questions; a mechanical activity which could be performed without an accurate understanding of the material involved. Edward's skill in this area indicated that he was capable of using his eyes fairly well in a reading situation. He possessed the mechanical means for becoming a good reader, but his experience with words and concepts was so small that his reading ability had not been allowed to develop. Verbal skills were also deficient, indicating the lack of any sort of word attack, either sight or phonic. No fluency in reading had been achieved. It seemed Edward was as close to being a nonreader as was possible for a youngster who had spent ten years in school.

Edward tested out as having unilateral dominance. He was left-handed, left-eyed, and left-footed. His physical co-ordination was reasonably good, although his movements were at times jerky. It seemed, however, that the jerky, quick movement of his hands or shoulders was more a gesture of impatience or a means of combating frustration than a physical compulsion. These movements were apparent only when Edward was talking or when he was trying to read. When he was quiet, he was absolutely immobile, his face perfectly expressionless, except for his eyes which seemed never to remain still.

Conference with School Counselor

Edward's counselor said that as far as the school was concerned they had tried, but they felt unable to make any further effort with him. He was allowed to attend classes if he wished, but none of his teachers felt that any purpose was being served by his presence in the classroom. On occasions, he would volunteer information during class discussions, but he was not really regarded either by his teachers or his fellow students as a member of any class. He went to school because there was nothing else for him to do. For the most part, he was well behaved in school, although at times he would be argumentative when talking to a teacher or anyone else in authority. The school expected that he would be withdrawn when he reached his sixteenth birthday. Edward's counselor seemed disinclined to discuss Edward's problems and difficulties. When pressed on any specific points, he said that he was unable to discuss the case. He said that there was no doubt but that the ability to read would be helpful to Edward, but he limited himself to vague generalizations. Edward, he said, had a long way to go, and he added it was the school's opinion that Edward would not be able to gain a high-school diploma.

Conferences with Parents

When Edward's mother first attended the conference, she wanted only to be assured that Edward had the mental capacity to learn to read. She said that his lack of ability to read had aggravated his other problems, and she and her husband felt that if he could learn to read with some success, there would be hope for him. She said he was very much interested in the drama class at high school and her husband had tried to encourage him in this direction by introducing him to a friend who worked in a local radio station. Edward, she said, spent a good deal of time at the radio station and had become acquainted with some of the announcers there. He had begun to worry increasingly, however, about his lack of reading ability, because he realized that to be an announcer, it was necessary to be a good reader. During the first conference with Edward's mother, little more information was provided than had been provided by the school.

A schedule of instruction was set up for Edward at the clinic. The intention was to start with basic phonics to provide him with some word-attack skills that might develop his confidence along with his reading skill.

After two weeks, when Edward had not appeared for any instruction, his parents were telephoned. A conference appointment was set up with Edward's father, and he appeared for the conference alone. He was a worried-looking man who did not expect that much could be done for Edward. During the first fifteen minutes of the conference, he spoke in generalities about Edward's continuing school difficulties. He wanted to know what sort of training was recommended.

When the father was asked why Edward had not attended the instruction sessions set up, he sighed deeply and then began to talk about the extent of Edward's problems. Edward, he said, was once again in a county juvenile home, but he would be released shortly. The situation, he felt, was becoming desperate, and neither he nor his wife knew which way to turn.

Edward had been under psychiatric care for over three years, and the psychiatrist felt that many of his more violent aggressive tendencies had been curbed, but he was unable to provide any assurance that Edward would ever be free of his excessive anxieties. The psychiatrist reported that Edward's intelligence level was slightly above average and he had the mental capacity to learn to read and perform satisfactorily in his academic subjects, but his emotional development had been so deficient that it was questionable whether he could ever perform as a mature person.

Four years prior to the conference, Edward had attended a remedial school for one school year. This school reported that his intelligence was high and that he had achieved academic skills equivalent to his grade level. At this point, Edward's father mentioned that Edward had been adopted at the age of three and that both parents had found him a constant worry from the beginning.

The father was particularly concerned about Edward's lack of confidence. He reported that in every activity, Edward seemed to make a feeble attempt and then give up. He had taken the boy to the mountains to learn to ski. They had both been novices, but the father seemed to catch on fairly rapidly. Edward grew discouraged quickly and refused to try after the first day. The father had cajoled him and encouraged him, but Edward had refused to make a further effort. The pattern of his performance in all things seemed to follow this sort of scheme. In his school work, this pattern had emerged early. If he did not meet with immediate success, he refused to participate.

Edward's father was told that the probability of the boy's achieving effective reading skills was doubtful until his other problems were straightened out. The important consideration was the strength of Edward's desire to learn to read; only if his motives were extremely strong could he be expected to make consistent progress. It was agreed that Edward would start his instructions at the clinic on an individual basis within the following week.

Conference with Student

Conferring with Edward was like trying to hold back a restive horse. His mind darted in all directions impelled by a flow of words. The words were, for him, an automatic cover to the fear and anxiety he felt as the result of having been asked to discuss his academic difficulties. Edward was a tall boy, physically mature. By his appearance, he might have been in his early 20's, but he seemed to lack the stability of someone half his true age. When talking, Edward shifted his gaze to his listener's face and then away, constantly. His words were hurried, but he spoke well, expressing himself intelligently and coherently.

He carried with him an assortment of papers, mostly teletype press dispatches that are received in radio stations. In the course of his monologue, he dipped into his pockets, rummaged around, and came up with odd scraps of these messages. He laid them in front of him and read a sentence or two. He also carried newspaper clippings with him. When asked to read one of the newspaper articles, he read the first sentence rapidly, then folded the paper and put it back in his pocket. Edward was asked to finish reading the article, but he ignored the request and went on talking about one of the radio announcers who did a thorough job of editing news dispatches. Edward said he realized one had to be good at English in order to do this editing, and that was why he wanted to study reading.

He was asked about his studies at school and why he did not seem able to complete any of his courses. He insisted that the school had just given up on him. He said they let him sit in class and he did not bother anyone, but whenever he raised his hand and wanted to say something, the teacher would not call on him. He supposed that they got a little annoyed when he shouted out what he had to say—". . . but then, why don't they call on me?"—he wanted to know. He said there were some students in the class who were even dumber than he was when it came to schoolwork. Some of them had not even opened their mouths all year, and a lot of times he knew the answers, but they would not call on him. But anyway, he said, he liked it at school—it was all right—as long as they did not bother him.

He was told that the school had offered to release him from classes to work on his reading at the clinic and that his parents felt that he was now willing to put forth sufficient effort to improve his reading. He became very serious and said that he would try very hard, because he knew how important it was.

Instruction Provided

Edward attended the clinic for a total of seven sessions. He was given basic phonic instruction on the blackboard which was supplemented by phonic exercises on the tachistoscope. His attention span was very short. He would seem to be making good progress, and while being taught seemed to grasp the principles involved, but half an hour later he failed to remember what he had learned. At times he would run his hand over his forehead as though he were in agony, then shake his head vigorously and say that he had forgotten. The next session consisted of a repetition of the preceding one, but each time Edward encountered the same material, it was new to him. After each small failure, he would expertly draw the instructor into conversation in order to distract him from the job at hand. Edward would launch into a rambling but intense account of some incident that had happened at school or at the radio station. He spoke quickly and had a natural dramatic sense for the stories he told, even though the stories were usually pointless. In his stories, he pictured himself in a competent, almost heroic, role. His need for the attention and approval of the instructor was so overt as to be embarrassing. The instructor reported he felt that perhaps it was as important for him to play the part of an interested audience as it was to insist on academic performance, even though he realized that Edward's need for attention was probably insatiable. At the conclusion of seven 2-hour sessions, Edward again stopped coming. An inquiry revealed that he was once again at the county juvenile home.

Conference with Parole Officer

About a month after Edward's instruction sessions had stopped, he was brought into the clinic for a conference by the parole officer from the juvenile home. Mr. H., the parole officer, was very sympathetic to Edward's problems but had few illusions as to the efficacy of any training. During the first part of the conference, Edward remained out in the waiting room. At this time, Mr. H. said that if Edward had received intensive individual training eight or nine years previously, some of his problems might never have developed. On the other hand, there could be no assurance that this would have been the case. Mr. H. believed that there was still a chance that Edward could be straightened out, and he felt very strongly that if Edward could develop reading skills, the boy's chances would be greatly improved. He said that about three-fourths of the youngsters who got into serious trouble with the law were found to be functional non-readers. As he explained it, these children lacked the means for making contact with society. Their lack of reading ability isolated them, keeping them from associations and work opportunities which might make them feel that they belonged to any community. Equally important, he said, was the fact that from an early age, the image that they created of themselves was of an incompetent and ineffectual person. Anyone with such an image of himself would seek ways to compensate and these ways were usually antisocial. Edward, Mr. H. maintained, possessed basic verbal dexterity which made him rely on the verbalization of his experiences in order to keep himself on an even keel emotionally. Since this was true, his failure to develop reading proficiency affected him

149

even more deeply than was true in other cases. Although Mr. H. was skeptical about the chances of Edward's overcoming his problems at so late a stage, he still felt that the effort was worth making.

Mr. H. explained that Edward's stepparents had always proved very co-operative. They were intelligent and sympathetic people who had really given Edward every possible chance to straighten himself out. They were a well-to-do couple and had provided every possible advantage for Edward from the moment he had come to them. His development had shocked them, and they tended to blame themselves for things over which they had had no control. However, Edward felt that both of them had in some subtle way conspired against him, and he seemed to resent everything they did for him just as he resented the fact that they were not his real parents.

Mr. H. then called Edward into the conference room and asked him point-blank whether he would concentrate on learning to read well. Mr. H. told him that this opportunity was being made available to him once again and everyone concerned had confidence in his ability to take advantage of it. His parents, the juvenile authorities, and the clinic were all ready to co-operate and to work with him. Edward said he was sure that he was ready to make the effort.

Edward failed to appear for the next scheduled instruction session. His parents were telephoned and it was reported that Edward had attacked his stepfather, then disappeared, and had finally been located. Certain criminal acts had been traced to him and he had been sent to a state correctional institution.

Case Study 12

Student: Dan R.

Age: 14

School Grade: 8 (End of Grade 8)

Initial Reading Score: Gr. 6.0

Hours of Instruction: 40

Diagnosis

Dan's initial test indicated a high level of verbal skills, but a poor retention of factual information and low interpretive ability. He read very slowly, and the lack of fluency seemed to contribute directly to poor comprehension skills. While taking the test, Dan went over the material again and again, his eyes darting all over the page. He attempted only those questions of which he was certain and was unwilling to commit himself on those questions about which he had any doubt. While being tested, he puzzled over each question for a lengthy period, then slumped in his chair and stared at the wall, his face impassive.

On the phonic test, he gave up very quickly after assuring himself that he was not able to cope with the material. He made a few desultory stabs at three or four questions and then gazed at the test, a worried expression on his face.

Probably as much was to be learned from the manner in which Dan attempted to take the test as the test results themselves. The scattered eye-movement pattern and lack of phonic knowledge suggested that he had been taught to read by the sight system, but he had been unable to achieve sufficient fluency to make his skills effective. On the other hand, his spelling was accurate, confirming the conclusion drawn from high scores on the verbal exercises that his visual retention was well above average. Ordinarily, a student who possesses as high a level of visual skill as Dan is able to develop good reading performance, unless (as seemed to be true in Dan's case) the habit of skipping unfamiliar words is allowed to develop. In such instances, a consistent eye-movement pattern is rarely developed, and consequently, a firm grasp of material is not easily achieved. Such a student may gain a general but vague idea of a passage, but the logic underlying a piece of written material calls for absorbing words and ideas in their sequential order. Dan's effective sight vocabulary was, therefore, of little help to him when it came to understanding and interpreting what he read.

As is almost invariably true with students who give evidence of good visual retention, Dan had strong unilateral dominance. He was right-eyed, right-handed, and right-footed. His physical co-ordination was excellent. He was particularly neat and tidy about his person as well as with his belongings. He moved gracefully and smoothly, and when he spoke, there was no hesitation. He wrote with good speed and formed his letters well. On the tachistoscopic test he displayed a very high level of visual retention and accuracy. There was no evidence of any physical obstacle to the development of good reading skills.

Reports from Schoolteachers

Dan had been in his present school for only a short time. His principal reported that his intelligence tests showed he possessed superior intelligence, but his grades were at a barely passing level. The principal had spoken to the school from which Dan had come, and the report of his previous teacher emphasized that Dan was not working anywhere near capacity. The principal said, however, that everyone who had come in contact with Dan had been impressed with his co-operative attitude and conscientiousness, but at the same time, they were concerned about his poor academic showing. It seemed that he had the ability and the desire to do well but was defeating himself for some series of complex, subconscious reasons, not as yet fully identified. The principal noted that Dan had not been a student in any school system other than the one from which he had just come. He said that Dan's present teachers felt that they did not know the boy sufficiently well to be able to provide much help, although one teacher had remarked that Dan, in class, seemed frequently to let his mind wander. His attention to what was going on in class was spasmodic. The school from which Dan had come had sent along to his present school a folder containing extensive special tests—both psychological and achievement—but the principal said there were no conclusive judgments to be drawn from this material except that his school had been sufficiently concerned about the evidences of high capacity and low performance to have sought some of the underlying causes. No work had been done by Dan with the school psychologist, but it was felt that if his academic performance continued at a low level, such a course would have to be recommended. The principal remarked that he was accustomed to youngsters of Dan's age rebelling, but he had rarely met with a rebellion which was so successfully hidden from the rebel himself.

Conference with Parent

This conference was attended by Dan's stepfather, who was deeply concerned about the boy's scholastic difficulties. The stepfather explained that he had married Dan's mother, a divorcée, about two years previously. Dan had seemed at all times happy with the relationship and was helpful and considerate at home. He was an only child and inevitably spent a good deal of time alone. When there was any sort of family activity, he participated willingly and showed no resentment. Dan's father was living in another part of the country and wrote to his son about once a month. Both Dan's stepfather and mother encouraged the boy to maintain the correspondence, and Dan did so. Before writing a letter to his father, he would generally ask his mother what he should say, and after the letter was written, he would show it to her or to his stepfather. He showed them, too, the letters from his father, which were chatty and pleasant. The stepfather said that every attempt had been made to treat the relationship in a natural manner.

The stepfather regretted that he was not able to spend as much time with Dan as he wished; unfortunately, Dan's mother and he were quite busy with social and business responsibilities which took them out of town frequently. When he went on a business trip, he generally wanted his wife to accompany him. At these times, Dan was left at home with the servants, who had been with the family for many years, but the stepfather realized that leaving the boy with servants was far from ideal, even though they were very fond of Dan and went out of their way to be helpful to him. He had wanted to take Dan on trips, but since the boy was doing so badly at school, he had been reluctant to have him miss any of his classes.

Before completing the conference, the stepfather mentioned that the boy's mother had wanted to attend the conference with him, but she had unfortunately been tied up with a previous engagement.

Conference with Student

Dan was attentive and interested at the conference, although he said nothing unless asked a direct question. He seemed well-poised, but a slight trembling of his hands indicated that he was under great tension. His answers to questions were polite. He seemed to make an effort to reply conscientiously to whatever questions he was asked, but he frequently answered that he was not sure or was unable to say. When the questions touched on his relationship with his family, he seemed to freeze up and answered mechanically.

He said his schoolwork was easy for him while he was in class, but when he went over it at home, he did not seem to be able to remember what he was responsible for. He liked his teacher and realized that she was interested in helping him. His principal had been very kind and had talked to him a number of times. He liked the school, but he did not know many of his classmates as yet. He had also liked the school he had attended previously. He was glad that his parents were sending him to the clinic, because he knew he needed help. In every respect, Dan was the most co-operative and pleasant student imaginable.

Dan was asked if he had any idea why it was so difficult for him to concentrate on his studies. He said he did not know; it just seemed that there was a kind of wall between him and the things he had to learn. He was asked if he found himself thinking of other things while he was supposed to be studying. He said that when he sat down to read a book, his mind just went blank.

The results of his diagnostic test were then discussed with Dan, and he was told that he would have to develop better word-attack skills and greater fluency in order to improve his comprehension. He nodded his head as though he understood perfectly. He was told that gaining reading skill was neither complicated nor difficult, particularly for someone whose verbal knowledge was as extensive as his; but no one could do it for him, and he would have to force himself to make a sustained effort. It was emphasized to him that the responsibility for his work was his alone and that although his low level of scholastic achievement made those close to him unhappy, it probably made him more unhappy than anyone else. Dan said he realized this and would work hard to improve.

Somehow his answers seemed designed more to please than to give information. He seemed to be using agreeableness as a curtain behind which he retired. The problem would be how to arouse sufficient interest in Dan himself to enable him to discard the defensive curtain.

Recommendations

In order to increase basic reading skill, it would be necessary for Dan to develop an effective method of word attack based on phonic knowledge. Intensive verbal-structure exercises would help him to develop an understanding of the relationship between words, and such an understanding would possibly lead to heightened interest in verbal activities. It would also be necessary for Dan to develop sufficiently consistent eye-movement patterns for the development of greater fluency. Increased comprehension could be expected once this fluency was his.

Since Dan tended to withdraw from any academic challenge that threatened his security, it was felt that putting him in a situation of a highly competitive nature might force him to accept such challenges, particularly if it were demonstrated to him that he could compete successfully. His visual skills were high, and there was no question but that he could do very well on the tachistoscopic exercises. Although he did not need this drill, it would still be desirable for him to engage in it, for he would be able to demonstrate to himself his skill as compared with his competing classmates. Such an experience might well help him to develop the confidence he needed.

Instruction Provided

Dan was assigned to work with a small group consisting of three other boys and a girl, all of whom were as intelligent as he, but performing at a higher level. Dan had difficulty initially in keeping up with the group, and supplementary acceleration exercises were given to him. He was also given special intensive work on phonics and word structure. At the conclusion of each activity, Dan reported his progress confidentially to his instructor (the instructor kept a careful record of his progress but made no comment). Every day's instruction started with tachistoscopic work. At the conclusion of this activity Dan was highly encouraged and in a suitable frame of mind to attack the assignments that were more difficult for him. The timed reading exercises with extensive comprehension-question material gave him the most trouble. His attention still tended to fade out after every few minutes of concentrated application. At such times, his instructor would ask him what difficulty he was encountering and would discuss the reading passage with him, providing encouragement.

After the first ten hours of training, the instructor was told to start grading Dan on each of his activities. His first reaction was to ask whether these grades would be sent home. When he was told they would not, he seemed puzzled, and it was explained to him that the grades were for his own guidance, so that he could see whether he was progressing as rapidly as he should. It was felt that Dan was possibly trying, subconsciously, to punish those closest to him, and at each stage the attempt was made to emphasize to him that his academic handicap was his problem and no one else's.

Dan began to respond to the competitive atmosphere. It was not long after training began that he became interested in the level of performance of his classmates. The group was made up of outgoing youngsters who talked freely among themselves about their performance on successive exercises. It took Dan some time before he joined in this chatter, but when he did, it was felt that a great stride had been taken.

Throughout his training, Dan was treated as an adult; no pressure was put on him; no judgment was overtly made on his work. His performance was allowed to speak for itself. Records were kept of what he did, but in a disinterested way. It was felt that this hands-off approach would motivate Dan most quickly, since it placed the initiative squarely on his own shoulders. During his school experience, he had, for many years, been told that he could do better if he tried. He had responded, it seemed, by feeling that as long as his teachers were worried about him, there was no need for him to worry about himself. The fact that his parents did not seem to be as much concerned about him as he probably felt they should, complicated the situation. On the one hand, he felt his teachers would do his worrying for him if he did not work and on the other hand, he felt he would be getting even with his parents by pursuing the same course. In some cases, this sort of situation would call for gaining the active co-operation of the parents, but there seemed little hope that the family relationship in Dan's case could be radically and quickly altered. More important, Dan seemed to be meeting the challenge offered him and was probably capable of accepting his responsibility at an adult level.

Progress Achieved

Dan attended the clinic for a total of forty hours. He did not begin to achieve any appreciable results until after the first twelve hours, at which point he spurted ahead remarkably. From this stage, his work settled down to a more steady pattern of achievement. His confidence grew slowly and his test performance remained very spotty, but his overall ability seemed to be growing along with his conviction that he was able to handle his schoolwork.

Dan was tested frequently in order to provide evidence for himself of the improvement he was making, and although the tests did not show consistent development of skills, they did demonstrate to him that effective school performance was within his grasp. His confidence in his ability began to grow, and his scholastic performance was on the way to improvement.

Case Study 13

Student: **Charles G.**

Age: **14**

School Grade: **8 (Middle of Grade 8)**

Initial Reading Score: **Gr. 9.5**

Hours of Instruction: **30**

Diagnosis

The diagnostic reading test was performed by Charles with intense concentration. His brows were knit into a frown and he grasped his pencil with great force. He worked through the questions methodically without wasting a moment, but each time he answered a question, he would quickly glance over it again to reassure himself. It seemed he had to make a great effort to leave one question before going on to the next, as though reluctant to tear himself away from the specific task at hand. As he read, his eyes kept going back to words already absorbed. Watching him read was in itself revealing; he displayed the compulsive reading pattern of the perfectionist who is never quite satisfied that he has grasped fully the meaning or import of a sentence or word. As a result, Charles's reading rate was very slow, but his retention of detailed factual information was high. Verbal skills, too, were at a high level. Charles was particularly knowledgeable with regard to the denotative meanings of words. He obviously had great familiarity with the dictionary and had pigeonholed words and definitions together. He was, therefore, able to perform successfully exercises requiring identification of words in isolation, but when he was called on to get general meanings from a given context, he fell down. He seemed unreceptive to the connotative aspects of language; he did not grasp underlying meanings or generalized inferences, and accordingly lacked the ability to interpret what he read.

Charles displayed the usual deficiencies associated with lack of reading fluency. He vocalized heavily, even to the point of moving his lips slightly; he read as though reading consisted of identifying words rather than ideas. It was necessary for Charles to piece together the isolated words in order to grasp the thought contained in sentences. This plodding, painful, inefficient method produced results which might have been expected: Charles learned about each tree, but he was unable to comprehend the forest.

Charles's concern with isolated words had made it necessary for him to develop a high degree of phonic knowledge, in spite of the fact that he had been taught to read through the sight system. Most of his phonic knowledge was not conscious, but he had figured out by himself the relationships between letters and their sounds in just about every variation. When faced with an unfamiliar word, Charles would sound it out, but haltingly, by syllables. This sort of phonic attack tended further to cut down Charles's reading speed and, concomitantly, his ability to grasp general concepts. Charles represented a student of first-rate capacity whose compulsive temperament had made of him a comparatively ineffectual performer.

Charles tested as right-eyed, right-handed, and right-footed. Unilateral dominance was strong and physical co-ordination satisfactory. However, when writing, Charles found himself the prey of a number of small involuntary movements. He would raise his pencil after writing a word in order to examine what he had written. He would then use his pencil as a pointer to guide his eyes in going back over the word he had just completed writing. When reading from printed material, he liked to hold a pencil in his hand to point at the words he was reading. When the pencil was taken from him, he used his finger. Although Charles gave every evidence of being driven by uncertainties while performing reading or writing functions, he still seemed to enjoy doing these activities and appeared completely wrapped up in them. The pattern of physical movements which accompanied reading and writing were intended as an unconscious reinforcement of his capacities, but the movements had become obstacles to smooth and efficient performance.

Conference with Schoolteacher

Charles's teacher said that she was very fond of him, although she could not bear to watch him work because of all the wasted motions which were an inevitable part of his doing anything. She reported that he was rarely able to complete an assignment, although he always did a remarkably thorough, accurate job on the part he did finish. According to school records, his intelligence was at a superior level, and the school expected him to make an excellent record if only he could be trained to relax and work more easily and with less tension. She felt that the basis of his difficulty lay in his lack of confidence in himself. She said that he seemed unable to let go of any task once he had started it, as though he were constantly making sure that there would be no grounds for criticism.

She knew Charles's mother and father and had also been the teacher of his older sister. The sister had not been at all like Charles. As a matter of fact, the sister had been, if anything, a somewhat careless worker and an easygoing child. Charles's father, however, was a man of tremendous drive. He was a successful lawyer, and Charles's teacher characterized him as "very dynamic." He was closely concerned with his son's academic achievement and would always accompany his wife when parent-teacher conferences were held. Charles's mother was, according to the teacher, a very pleasant, amiable person who said little when with her husband, allowing him to do the talking.

Conference with Parents

Charles's mother and father both attended the conference. Charles's father asked specific questions with regard to Charles's reading performance. He seemed dismayed that Charles was not a superior reader, and it appeared that he felt the difficulties Charles was experiencing in getting through his schoolwork were a reflection on himself. He was genuinely concerned, but at the same time kept repeating that he could not understand why the boy was so slow.

The findings of the diagnostic test were explained to him, and it was pointed out that Charles gave every evidence of lacking confidence in his own ability and compensated by trying never to make a mistake. Charles's father wanted to know what could be done. He was told that a program would be set up with the aim of making Charles into a superior reader. It would not be wise or possible to try to make him less careful in his work, but at the same time, it was felt that he could be trained to work with greater fluency.

Charles's mother said that she could not understand why the boy should lack confidence; his grades were reasonably high. The only thing that bothered her was the amount of time he had to spend on his homework. He came home from school and went directly to his room where he stayed, studying until dinnertime. Immediately after dinner, he returned to his room and worked until midnight. He often got up early in the

163

morning to go over the assignments he had worked on the night before, so that they would be fresh in his mind for school.

Charles's father interrupted his wife to say that he had no objection to his son applying himself so strenuously to his work. What he objected to was that the boy seemed to accomplish so little considering the amount of time he put in. Charles's father remarked that at this rate the boy would never be able to handle the volume of work which he would encounter when he got to college. Charles's mother said she could not understand why her son was such a perfectionist. She said no one had ever put any pressure on him; he had never been made to feel that he would be punished if he did not do well, and the father agreed with her. He added that if the boy were not capable, then he would not mind, but he hated to see a bright youngster waste his talents.

Charles's mother said that Charles did not have much time for friends but that he did have one close friend and they were often together on week ends, usually at Charles's house. They rarely attended school functions and did not participate in athletic or club activities. The principal of the school had called both parents into his office about three months before and asked that they encourage Charles to engage in some extracurricular work. The parents had discussed the question with Charles, but he had agreed with his father that his studies must receive priority. Charles had complained that he must be very stupid if his homework took him so much time, and this had upset both parents who realized that there should have been sufficient time for the boy to do his schoolwork and to pursue outside interests, too.

Conference with Student

Charles spoke very little. He quietly listened but volunteered no information. He responded only to direct questions and

164

then with a nod of his head or a murmur of concurrence. When asked whether or not he thought he could be taught to work more rapidly, he was noncommittal. When asked whether his lack of speed was a handicap to performance of his schoolwork, he said he guessed maybe it was. He seemed anxious to avoid taking a definite stand; he appeared intent on not committing himself to any course of action at which he might fail. When asked about his hobbies, he said he liked building model railroads and had an H.O. railway system in the basement. He was asked to describe his railway system and he said he had fixed part of it to look like a port with model ships in it. Behind the port were mountains which he had made of plaster of Paris and sprayed with green paint. For trees he had taken twigs and dipped them in varnish. He grew quite talkative telling about his trains, and then went on to relate in some detail the plans he had to extend the system if he could find enough time. He was asked if his parents ever helped him with the trains, and he said that his father was very much interested in them and would often make suggestions, but most of the ideas he had figured out for himself.

Recommendations

In order to provide Charles with a greater degree of confidence in his ability to handle his academic assignments, it would be necessary to develop his reading skills to a very effective level. The primary aim of any training would be to increase his rate of speed and also bring comprehensive skills to a high level. It was felt that before Charles would accept the fact of his own competence, he would have to be working so well that even *he* recognized his ability. By achieving excellent skills, it was hoped that Charles would begin to feel secure; only then could it be expected that the compulsive pattern of his performance might be changed. Only when Charles was operating

165

at a high peak of efficiency would he be able to demonstrate to himself daily that he was capable of meeting the challenges that he encountered.

Charles's basic capacity was very high, and it was felt that the desired level of skills would best be achieved by concentrating on an increased reading rate. Once reasonable fluency was established, understanding could be expected to improve. Some retraining of word-attack skills was indicated to help free Charles of his habits of excessive vocalization. A program was set up which combined visual training, acceleration, and comprehension exercises that had been designed primarily for development of interpretive skills.

Instruction Provided

Charles attended the clinic for a total of thirty hours over a period of seven-and-a-half weeks. During this time, he worked very hard on tachistoscopic exercises which were limited to verbal targets. Phrase material was flashed on the screen; the phrases used grew progressively longer. The purpose of these exercises was to increase eye span as well as cut down on the duration of each fixation. Eye-movement acceleration exercises were administered during each session and the speed was advanced, gradually at first. Once Charles grew accustomed to the devices, he was subjected to shock tactics on the eye-movement accelerator. He was given exercises at grade level, the speed of which was just a bit faster than was comfortable for him. He would then be given an exercise which used material two or three years below his level. This material would be presented at a speed one hundred words per minute faster than his normal reading speed. This exercise was followed immediately by grade-level material at a reduced rate. This method helped to move Charles out of the plodding pattern of eye movement and vocalization that had become habitual with him.

At the same time, work on an individual pacing device complemented the eye-movement acceleration. The pacer forced Charles to work more rapidly in a situation which more closely approximated normal reading. He was then assigned a selection to be read normally, but under timed conditions. In each of these three reading situations (eye-movement acceleration, pacing, and normal timed-reading), the material used with Charles alternated between easy material at high speeds and more difficult material at speeds which were slower, but still faster than his normal rate.

The word-attack exercises were aimed at freeing Charles from the habit of analyzing a word by mouthing it, syllable by syllable. A review of the basic phonic rules was first undertaken and then each unfamiliar word encountered was attacked with reference, first, to its initial sound, and then to each succeeding vowel sound. The word as a whole then had to be pronounced. The sounding out of unfamiliar words had to be made a mental rather than an oral process.

The comprehension exercises consisted of brief passages which were accompanied by timed question materials. Both the reading of the passages and the answering of the questions had to be accomplished within a prescribed time limit. Additional comprehension exercises required that Charles scan a brief paragraph and then write, in his own words and in one sentence, a resumé. Emphasis toward the latter part of Charles's clinic work was placed on the perfection of scanning techniques. He was taught how to identify key words and phrases and how to uncover the structure of a piece of writing by isolating the major ideas and listing under them the subsidiary details.

Prereading exercises were also given to Charles to provide practice in quickly discovering the general meaning and intent contained within a passage. After having preread a selection, Charles was asked to write a brief précis of the passage.

Close attention to note-taking procedures supplemented this work and provided additional practice in identifying important idea elements as well as the overall structure of written material.

Progress Achieved

Charles worked quite hard to develop his reading speed. It was not in his nature to be careless about understanding what he read, and the increased fluency which he developed enabled him to establish more effective interpretive skills. His attack on new words was made less conscious and labored and, therefore, more rapid.

Visual training and acceleration work forced Charles beyond a speed at which he could vocalize comfortably, although with challenging material he tended to revert to a slower speed, since he could not free himself completely of the habit of vocalizing. He seemed to require the sound of the words in his ears to help him understand difficult material, but even though he would say the words to himself, he was still able to do so at a much greater speed than had been the case before training. His understanding of what he read improved also.

It will take a considerable period of time before the increased reading skills which Charles possesses will contribute to development of greater confidence. Other important factors have still to be overcome, but being able to work with greater ease will surely help Charles revise the image he has of himself as an ineffectual student; one who must check over his work endlessly to assure himself that he is not making stupid errors, which, in his own mind, make him vulnerable to criticism.

Case Study 14

Student: James A.

Age: 14

School Grade: 7 (Middle of Grade 7)

Initial Reading Score: Gr. 4.3

Hours of Instruction: 58

Diagnosis

On his initial diagnostic reading test, James performed at
about three years below grade level. He had been taught to read
through a sight method and his word-attack skills were nonexistent. Visual perception, however, was of a high order and
retention of visual images was accurate. He read very slowly,
however, since his recognition vocabulary was so small and
he was able to comprehend very little of what he read. Phonic
knowledge was nonexistent except for the basic consonant
sounds. Reliability of the test was in doubt, since it was impossible to determine how serious an effort James had made in
taking the test. Other evidence had to be relied upon. A personal conference provided the most valuable information, although a discussion with his schoolteacher was also helpful.
A conference with James's mother served to throw additional
light on his problem.

At the time the silent-reading test was administered to

169

James, he was also tested for dominance. He had strong right laterality. He was physically well co-ordinated, alert, active, and decisive in his movements. There was present no indication of any physical obstacles to the development of effective reading skills.

Conference with Schoolteacher

James's teacher reported that although James gave every evidence of possessing superior intelligence, his academic performance was at so low a level that she had long since been forced to ignore his presence in class for the sake of the other children. He was a disruptive element in the classroom, played the clown, and interrupted her frequently with irrelevancies. When she attempted to discipline him or reason with him, he became surly and truculent. He did not challenge her authority overtly but in a variety of disingenuous ways. He seemed to be acting under a compulsion to distract both the teacher and the class in order to draw attention to himself. His teacher also reported that since he was very bright, spoke well, and had a particularly sharp sense of humor, he was frequently successful in making the class laugh. Having achieved such a success, he seemed gratified and would often, after such triumphs, enter seriously into class discussions for a brief time. His teacher said she was unhappy about James since she felt his obviously superior abilities were being wasted, but she felt that enlisting his co-operation was beyond her, and she only wished he would be taken from her classroom.

Conference with Parent

James's mother was a self-assured, competent woman. She had been divorced from James's father when the boy was ten years old, and although she was puzzled by James's attitude and angered by it, there was a strong emotional attachment between her and her son. She worked all day, holding down a responsible position and earning a high salary. Her job was demanding, and, she explained, kept her away from home for long hours. She tried to compensate for this by devoting almost all of her leisure time to James. They went to the movies together, frequently watched television shows together, and when she was able to cajole him into attempting his homework, she sat with him, helping. He had household chores for which he was responsible, but he rarely did them without her bringing pressure to bear. When she arrived home from the office at 6:00 P.M., after having asked him to vacuum the rugs or put the potatoes on to boil, she would frequently find him stretched out on the floor listening to rock 'n' roll music on the radio or thumbing through automobile magazines. The only other person who spent any amount of time at home with James was his maternal grandmother who had been widowed many years previously. James had not seen his father for two years. His mother reported that James had few friends and very rarely brought any other boy home. She realized he was not a popular child, and she was worried about his loneliness. She was more worried though by his seeming lack of energy, saying that he seemed to spend most of his time sitting and gazing out a window. He seemed to have little interest in anything and scarcely ever became absorbed in an activity or project.

Conference with Student

The most striking feature about James was his speaking vocabulary and his ability to express himself. He was highly articulate but used his verbal skill primarily to defend himself. He complained mildly about his mother and all the jobs she made him do around the house. There was no bitterness in him when he spoke of his mother and he mentioned her almost apologetically. He reserved his bitterness, however, for the house and the jobs for which he was responsible, and spoke with great contempt of the housework he was supposed to perform. When talking about school, he shrugged his shoulders constantly, as though trying to shake off the thought of his school experiences. He answered questions about his academic work noncommittally and accused his teacher of "not knowing the score." He agreed though, that some of the children in his class were pretty sharp, even if they did play up to the teacher; but, for most of his peers, he expressed contempt. When he spoke, his lip curled into an incongruous sneer. The incongruity stemmed from the fact that he was somewhat small for his age and had a delicate, almost pretty, face. He could assume an expression of innocence with great ease.

He refused to respond at all when questioned about his father.

His grandmother, he said, was "OK," but he would not specify in which way.

He displayed almost studied indifference about his schoolwork, as though it had no relationship to him at all. When asked what he thought he was at school for, he answered that it was not his idea to be there. When it was pointed out to him that he was reading three years below his grade level, he replied that that seemed pretty good, because he thought he was even worse at reading than that. He had constructed a thoroughly consistent and seemingly effective defense against the challenges he was having to meet. James had withdrawn, it seemed, from most of life.

Recommendations

Underneath the carefully constructed veneer of indifference displayed by James, there resided severe anxiety about his inabilities. The very elaborateness of the defensive wall provided some evidence of his apprehension. It was suggested to his mother that psychological help be sought. It was also suggested that an effort be made to provide James with some masculine influences. At the same time, James's mother was told that special instruction in reading should be started to give him basic tools for attacking his academic problems with some measure of success. It was pointed out that any student operating at his low level scholastically encountered a series of failures each day in school, and these failures inevitably contributed to his desire to withdraw from a world in which he was ineffectual. Emphasis in any reading training program would be placed first on the building of word-recognition skills emphasizing phonics. At the same time, visual capacity would be further developed. The aim in concentrating on word-attack skills would be to build an effective bridge between his speaking and his reading vocabularies. It was decided that he be assigned a man teacher, at least for this special work at the clinic. It was also suggested that the school assign him to a class taught by a man.

Instruction Provided

Before work with James could be initiated with any hope of achievement, it was necessary to gain his participation. His instructor was told that James was to be treated as though he were an adult; never was he to be attacked or dressed down. In the beginning, the instructor assigned a specific brief task for James to accomplish. James was told that the work would be checked in ten minutes and he was left in a study cubicle to do it himself. At the end of the ten minutes, the instructor returned to find that James had done nothing. Not a word of reproach was spoken. James was assigned another ten-minute task and left to himself to accomplish it. When the instructor returned, James had done nothing, but this fact was overlooked and he was assigned another task. The entire procedure was

173

impersonal, friendly, relaxed, and without overt pressure of any sort. This went on for four or five 2-hour sessions in the course of which James attempted no work. He had, however, begun to show some interest in the tachistoscopic exercises. His visual skills were excellent, and although he refused to participate—instead, he would write in his exercise book—when the visual images flashed on the screen, he did start to watch the screen when the flashes were due to appear. Soon he began to lean over to see what a neighboring student had written in response to a flash. Not long after this, he began to comment on this neighboring student's performance, saying aloud whether or not the other student had perceived the flash accurately. The other student responded by commenting that if James were so good, why didn't he write down what he saw. Feeling secure in his ability in this activity, James began to participate. This was the first small breakthrough. In a sense, it made James a member of the student body. He reacted very much as he did in school and reverted to the role of clown. If his disruption of the group activities was not severe, no word was said, but on occasions, James managed to interrupt the entire proceedings. At such times, he was asked to go to a room to see the director, who, by arrangement, was elsewhere. James was allowed to sit in the room for as long as half an hour, at the end of which time—without having been spoken to by anyone—he was asked to rejoin the group. Since his disruptive activities within the group were generally aimed at attracting attention and since he could attract no attention when isolated, this treatment was effective in reducing his clowning.

Within a short time after James began receiving special instruction in reading, his schoolteacher called to report that he was absenting himself from school frequently, evidently feeling that by receiving special instruction, he was thereby relieved from attendance at school. The principal of his school was consulted and it was decided that although his mother should be

174

informed, the school would not bring specific pressure to bear upon him for a while at least.

James's success in tachistoscopic work began to spark some interest in learning. He had not before experienced any kind of successful achievement in an academic context. On top of this, the responsibility for learning was shifted squarely onto his own shoulders for the first time in his life. There was no opportunity for him to justify his failure to perform on the grounds that it was something his teacher wanted him to do, rather than something he wished to do himself. At this point, James had to decide whether being alive and active was worth the effort. The treatment he had received demonstrated to him that if *he* didn't care, no one else did. He chose to participate and asked the instructor how he could figure out words that he did not know. Intensive training in phonic skills was undertaken immediately. It was pointed out to James that his extensive speaking vocabulary would be extremely helpful in building his reading vocabulary. It was demonstrated to him that most of the words written on a page were words that he recognized when they were spoken to him. By relating the letters in a word to the sounds produced by these letters, he could develop a means for identifying unknown words. After an initial period of confusion, James grasped the basic concepts, and once he had learned that a hitherto strange word could be sounded out, he grew deeply interested. A start had been made. Within the following weeks, James's understanding skills were strengthened as he was introduced to reading and comprehension exercises—initially at fourth-grade level but growing progressively more difficult. His mind seemed to be awakening as his reading skills developed, and one day he brought an article from a national magazine to his instructor. James had underlined the words he could not figure out. He was now reaching toward material at his mental level and was quickly gaining possession of sufficient skill to read those things which interested him.

Progress Achieved

After a total of fifty-eight hours of special instruction, James's reading skills tested out at grade level. Certainly his problems were far from being solved, but he was better equipped to accept his academic responsibility and thereby release the pressures which developed as the result of his daily failures at school. James's teacher at school reported that he was participating in classroom work and was beginning to turn in at least some homework assignments. James's mother reported that through the school's psychological services, James had become active with a group of boys interested in racing diminutive sports cars (Go-Karts). The group used the school grounds under supervision. Although he was not the most popular member of the group, he was at least accepted by the others and even had two of them visit at his home.

Section D—Disorganized Reading and Study Habits

Many highly capable students are unable to do their schoolwork at a level consistent with their ability. For the most part, these students have never developed skill in organizing their ideas into a coherent pattern. As a result, their retention of material is vague and inexact. In some cases, these students work at a painfully slow pace and they must struggle constantly to transform isolated words into ideas. They must then struggle further to create a logical pattern of the isolated ideas which they have extracted from their reading assignments. These students invariably have only one reading speed and one study approach. Whether they are reading a newspaper or a physics assignment, they start with the first word and, speaking the words to themselves as they go, attempt to squeeze whatever meaning they can from the words encountered. An efficient reader, on the other hand, has at his command a versatile approach, comprised of a variety of reading techniques. He is able to read rapidly and smoothly when he needs to or he scans and prereads where such methods are called for. He is able to take brief but meaningful notes on his reading, and he is able to organize the material he reads into a clear and logical

177

pattern. Study skills are properly related to reading skills. The inefficient reader cannot be an effective student.

Almost any student who is an average reader can, with training, become an excellent reader. He can expect to increase his reading speed and to develop excellent scanning techniques which will enable him to cover suitable material very rapidly. Many students, after learning to read with excellent comprehension at speeds in excess of six or seven hundred words a minute, are able to learn to scan thousands of words a minute with surprisingly good retention. It is rare to find a student who has received no special training in reading and study skills whose performance can compare with that of a trained reader.

The case histories which follow are intended to dramatize this fact and to provide evidence of the value to every student of a reading program.

Case Study 15

Student: **Susan D.**

Age: 17

School Grade: 12 (Middle of Grade 12)

Initial Reading Score: Gr. 13.6

Hours of Instruction: 24

Diagnosis

Susan was a B-plus student, but she spent two hours to complete one hour's work. Her initial test showed a high level of academic skills. Verbal ability, comprehension, and interpretive achievement were all high. A close examination of the test indicated that if she had been able to work more rapidly, her showing throughout the test would have been improved considerably. She scored in the top quarter of her grade level on comprehension and study skills, despite the fact that her reading rate was measured only at the twentieth percentile. (At the completion of her training, after only twenty-four hours of intensive work, when her reading rate had been increased to the sixty-fourth percentile, her comprehension and study skills tested out in the top twentieth of her grade level.)

Her very slow reading rate indicated that Susan was vocalizing heavily and reading without sufficient fluency to enable her to grasp connotative meanings or to interpret material quickly or reliably. Comparatively low interpretive scores indicated a need for training in grasping implied meanings and in organizing ideas into coherent patterns. Susan's grasp of underlying meanings could best be strengthened through emphasis on the structural aspects of reading material. Major concepts would have to be swiftly identified by her and the subsidiary ideas arranged under them. Attention to these factors, when coupled with exercises aimed at increasing speed and smoothness of reading, can lead to greatly improved study habits.

Susan scored well on the phonics survey. Her knowledge of the structure of words was adequate, but her attack on words, as indicated by her score on the vocabulary section of the test, was halting and painful. She worked accurately on this part of the test but completed relatively few of the questions. Susan's use of her phonic knowledge was not a fluent, automatic response, but rather a laborious breaking down of words into their phonic elements. She relied on her phonic knowledge when meeting unfamiliar words, but sounding out words was a conscious, slow process for her. Also, her sight vocabulary needed enlargement, and the ability to read for ideas rather than words had to be developed. Her poor showing on the contextual-meaning section of the diagnostic test indicated that her lack of fluency was probably also interfering seriously with her ability to grasp the meanings contained in complex sentences.

Susan was in need of developmental training that would help her to marshal the high level of skills she possessed in order to make them effective tools for academic achievement.

Susan tested out as right-eyed, right-handed and right-footed. No co-ordinational problems interfered with the development of reading skills. She was a neat, careful worker, overly conscientious about her schoolwork. She had developed compulsive eye-movement habits which were the result of temperament rather than of co-ordinational malfunction. The excessive backtracking and dwelling habits found in her eye-movement pattern had probably been developed as the result of her desire to absorb every bit of information contained in her reading. Such eye-movement habits are frequently associated with mixed-dominance problems, stemming from a basic inability to identify and retain visual images with ease. But in Susan's case, there was no evidence to indicate that her difficulty emanated from this source.

Conference with Schoolteacher

Susan's teacher was surprised to learn that Susan was seeking special training in reading. The girl's scholastic record was high; she had been well recommended by all of her teachers for entrance to the college of her choice. Her intelligence tests showed her to have a superior intellectual capacity. Her achievement showed her to be working at above seventieth percentile. The teacher, therefore, felt that Susan was not in need of improvement. It was pointed out to the teacher that Susan complained that her schoolwork occupied all of her leisure time and that she felt herself unprepared to tackle the heavy volume of academic work which she expected to encounter in college. It was also pointed out that with increased skills her achievement tests might well show an increase of anywhere from ten to fifteen percentile points, since she was unable to complete any demanding tests comfortably. The teacher's attitude was skeptical, but she said she would be happy to be kept informed of Susan's work at the clinic.

Conference with Parent

Susan's father was intensely interested in her progress. He was a highly educated, intelligent man whose own academic career had been distinguished. He felt that Susan should be

181

given every possible advantage for enabling her to excel in her school life. He said that it pained him to find Susan often studying doggedly until 1:30 or 2:00 o'clock in the morning. He was concerned that her social and emotional development was being impaired by what he considered to be her excessive attention to schoolwork. He remarked that considering the amount of energy she applied to academic assignments, her results, though good, should be even better. He remarked also that Susan was growing exceedingly tense with the frustrations she was experiencing at having to go over her work so many times. Reading a book was no real pleasure for her when she found it necessary to reread many passages if she wished to grasp the more profound meanings. He was curious to know at what speed Susan read, and was told that in material of average difficulty for her grade, Susan's rate was about 165 words per minute. He then asked at what speed Susan should be reading to accomplish her work effectively, and was told that effective readers at the high school level read at many different speeds, depending upon their assignments. They would generally read their narrative materials at speeds in excess of 450 or 500 words per minute. But it was emphasized to him that the lack of speed was not in itself as serious as the effect that regressive eye movements and halting reading habits had on the ability to organize and comprehend challenging material.

Susan's father apologized for the fact that his wife had not been able to attend the conference. She, too, was intensely interested in Susan's progress. He requested that a detailed report of initial test results be provided, so that both parents could discuss them with Susan and assure her of their interest in the training she was to take. He said he wanted to be able to provide whatever encouragement he possibly could. He knew from experience that any intensive training program tended at times to make a student feel inadequate to the task and discouraged about his ability to complete the program successfully. At such times, genuine interest and assurances from parents could prove valuable.

Conference with Student

Susan was a shy and inarticulate girl. She volunteered little information but answered questions put to her succinctly. There was an air of competence about her. She followed what was said to her closely, as though afraid to miss something. She was particularly worried about the scholastic demands that would be made on her when she attended college in the fall. She was assured that her abilities were at a level which would enable her to complete college work successfully, but it was pointed out to her that by increasing her reading and study skills, she would be able to approach college-level work with greater confidence and accomplish it with increased ease. The test results were discussed with her in detail and every effort was made to acquaint her intimately with the program which she was to embark on. The reasons for the exercises she would take were explained and the goals to be accomplished were outlined. It was felt that maximum achievement could be expected only if Susan herself was conscious of the aims as well as the methods of the program.

Susan was particularly interested in the means whereby her reading speed could be increased. She spoke with awe of her father's ability to get through printed material rapidly and added with some surprise that he remembered everything he ever read. She knew she would never read as well as he, but at least she wanted to be better at it than she was. She remarked wistfully that her father was terribly smart, and unless she was at the top of her class, he would be disappointed.

Susan was told that she had a basic capacity for high achievement and that she was fortunate that her parents were as much interested in her development of that capacity as they were.

Her father, she was told, was not unrealistic in his expectations, and she would really be happy with herself only when she was performing at the highest level of which she was capable.

Recommendations

Special training for Susan would emphasize increasing both reading speed and analysis of unfamiliar words. Once her basic reading rate had been increased to beyond three hundred words per minute, a program of study skills based on textbook material would be introduced, including practice in prereading, scanning, note-taking, and précis-writing. By the latter portion of the brief and intensive program, material of greater complexity would be utilized. Throughout the training, close attention would be paid to the development of verbal skills. Drill on prefixes, suffixes, and roots would familiarize Susan with the structure of words and further increase the effectiveness of her word attack.

With reference to the mechanical aspects of her reading ability, it was felt that through training with the eye-movement accelerator she should be broken of her regressive habits as quickly as possible. It was expected that once adequate speed had been achieved, the strongly ingrained vocalizing habits would also disappear.

It was felt that an intensive daily program totaling twenty-four hours of training would go a long way toward helping Susan become a more effective student.

Instruction Provided

Initially, Susan was exposed to extensive tachistoscopic work in order to increase visual capacity and to speed up co-ordination between eye and mind. This training was designed to

184

increase confidence in her ability to see accurately in order to help break her of the habit she had developed of going back to look at words again and again. It was expected that through phonic analysis of words encountered in the tachistoscopic exercises, Susan would also learn to speed up her word attack. Up until this time, she had been using her phonic knowledge ineffectively. Every strange word encountered was sounded out by her orally, letter by letter and syllable by syllable. It was necessary that she learn how to identify the sounds in her mind and to arrive at a grasp of unfamiliar words automatically and almost instantaneously. The tachistoscopic exercises were restricted to verbal material. At first, single words were flashed. As the training progressed, short phrases and then longer phrases were introduced. Throughout all the tachistoscopic work, challenging terms were isolated for phonic analysis. In this analysis, the vowel elements were identified first and then the entire word was identified.

At the same time as the tachistoscopic work was being carried on, Susan was given exercises on the eye-movement accelerator. Here again the development of eye-mind co-ordination was one of the major aims. The text material was masked by the reading device in a left-to-right direction. If Susan failed to see a word or phrase because of attempts to regress, she would lose the trend of an entire sentence. She soon learned to keep up with the masking mechanism. As soon as she gave evidence of being able to comprehend material effectively at a given speed, the rate was increased.

Adult-level reading exercises with comprehension questions were introduced into Susan's program within six hours after her initial session. She was allowed a limited amount of time to complete these exercises; a factor which helped rid her of the compulsive habits, which had become so much a part of her overall reading pattern, of rechecking her work.

Exercises on the reading pacer supplemented the eye-movement training and prepared Susan for normal, timed-reading activities.

When twelve hours of training had been completed, study-skill techniques were introduced. A fixed pattern of activities was established. The teaching process paralleled that described for Eleanor W. on pages 192-199.

It was pointed out to Susan that the particular study techniques which she was using were not necessarily applicable to all material, but when she dealt with technical or highly factual assignments, these techniques were recommended. She was also assured that after she had gone through a number of these exercises, she would want to adjust the method to suit specific study assignments. She could take shortcuts and in other ways modify the techniques, but while learning, it was wise for her to follow the prescribed pattern.

The main purpose of the study-skills training was to teach Susan to organize material as it was read and to equip her to handle complex assignments with greater hopes of success.

Vocabulary work emphasizing verbal structure was made an integral part of each day's work. The vocabulary activities were based on the particular verbal demands made by the selections read during that session. By setting up a word-attack pattern based on verbal structure, derivations, and phonic analysis, useful habits were established and a deeper interest in words was developed.

Progress Achieved

The twenty-four-hour program completed by Susan was very intensive. She attended the clinic two hours a day for a total of twelve days during a school vacation. In any training program of such short duration, the question of how well the student retains the skills achieved is of primary concern. Since reading training has as its purpose the establishment of firm reading habits which become a part of the student's arsenal, the most effective schedule would call for brush-up sessions at intervals over a period of many months. Only in this way is it possible to insure continued development of skills. In those cases where brush-up training is difficult to schedule, it is essential that the student be willing, on his own, to continue practicing the skills developed. Timed exercises with accompanying question material should be undertaken at least three or four times a week for a period of three to six months following training, and the study techniques learned should be employed conscientiously on homework assignments.

In Susan's case, continued home practice was carried out, and Susan's father reported, six months after completion of the program, that Susan's academic achievement had reflected the improvement he had hoped for. She was working, he said, at her capacity and faced college with greater confidence.

Case Study 16

Student: Eleanor W.

Age: 16

School Grade: 11 (End of Grade 11)

Initial Reading Score: Gr. 13.0

Hours of Instruction: 30

Diagnosis

Eleanor's diagnostic test revealed that her reading skills were of a very high order. The only area in which work was indicated was "Rate." Her top reading speed was about 350 to 375 words per minute, a speed which, considering her scholastic accomplishment, represented a handicap, since it took her longer to complete her school assignments than should have been necessary. However, her speed was sufficient to indicate that she should be able to exceed the vocalizing barrier and begin to read with her eyes and mind, without vocalizing the words as she read. Eleanor's school grades were all A's and B's. Her grades in English, History, and Social Studies, which required extensive reading, were mostly A's. She had one year of high school to complete before going on to an Eastern college, and she was concerned about her ability to take full advantage of a college education. She recognized that on a com-

188

parative basis, she spent more time completing her work than was necessary.

The phonic survey test given to Eleanor revealed a few areas of deficiency. She was of that generation which had received no phonic training in the primary and elementary grades. The phonic principles she knew had been figured out by her in the course of her gaining verbal experience, since she had a natural aptitude for understanding the basic structure of words; however, her understanding had not been consciously achieved, with the result that in some instances she was confused about pronunciation and spelling of unfamiliar terms.

Watching Eleanor take the diagnostic test provided some further information. She worked quickly but refused to move on to the next question until she had thoroughly completed the one under attack. She was keyed up while taking the test. The marks on her examination folder were very black; she bore down heavily on her pencil and her face was set in a deep frown. She was one of those people who seemed to work well under tension, but the probability existed that if she were working on demanding academic activities for a sustained period, the high nervous pressure, exerted constantly for a long time, would be fatiguing and would begin to interfere not only with her academic work but with her entire outlook. It seemed essential that Eleanor be given the chance to develop so high an order of reading and study skills that she would be able to perform her work without the anxiety which characterized her approach.

Eleanor tested out as a unilateral right dominant. Her physical co-ordination was excellent. She moved gracefully, though she tended to be a trifle careless about her person. This carelessness was reflected in her handwriting. She wrote with a fluent, rapid hand, but her writing varied frequently and the slant of it changed markedly, depending upon the amount of pressure she felt herself to be under. When she was bearing down heavily on the paper, the letters stood straight up and down, and when the writing was spidery and fine, the letters tended to lean to the left. The writing done under pressure was more accurate than the relaxed writing. The latter contained instances in which Eleanor had left out letters or even whole syllables, and in some cases, she had substituted an *l* for a *b* or *h* for *t*. The pattern of these errors was consistent with Eleanor's general disposition. She seemed to be an easygoing girl who was, however, particularly susceptible to academic pressure and sensitive about not performing at capacity. When relaxed she tended to display to an extreme degree the easygoing, careless aspects of her nature; when under pressure, however, she grew fearful of not doing well and performed accurately and effectively.

Conference with School Counselor

Eleanor's counselor felt that the girl had an exceptional academic future, but she was worried about the tensions and anxieties exhibited by Eleanor about the completion of her academic work. It was the counselor who had referred Eleanor to the clinic for special instruction. She hoped that by achieving a high level of reading skill, some of Eleanor's tensions might be relaxed. The counselor said that although Eleanor's grades at school were excellent, it had to be remembered that as she headed for college, her grades and performance would be judged by more demanding standards. Throughout her school career, Eleanor's performance in class and on tests had been gauged in accordance with the performance of the students in the school. Of this entire group, however, only about 20 per cent possessed the capacity to complete a top-level college program. When Eleanor's grades, tests, and aptitudes were judged in comparison with this gifted group, the margin of her superiority was not as impressive. It was the counselor's

190

task to make clear to Eleanor the realities of her situation. She would be expected, she was told by the counselor, to meet severe competition in the college she planned to attend, and although she could approach her college career with confidence, since she had the ability to do well, it was important that she not overlook the areas in which her preparation might be improved upon.

Conference with Parents

Both of Eleanor's parents attended the conference. Her mother was a large, efficient woman who spoke in a loud and confident voice, but she spoke sense, being fully aware of Eleanor's strengths and weaknesses. The father, although a quiet man, seemed to control the home situation. When he started to speak, whether or not his wife was in the middle of a sentence, she grew quiet. They were both college graduates and Eleanor's father was an architect, having been at one time a teacher at a nearby university. Eleanor had two older brothers and a younger sister. One brother had completed his college training and was doing graduate work in architecture, and the other brother was a Junior at an Eastern college. The family as a whole was academically gifted, and Eleanor had grown up in an atmosphere in which it had been assumed that she would make a superior scholastic record.

It was pointed out to Eleanor's parents that a developmental reading program including study-skills training could make her a superior reader. She could be expected to achieve speeds in the neighborhood of one thousand words a minute with good understanding on some types of material, and she could be trained to scan material of average difficulty at speeds of three thousand to four thousand words per minute, grasping about 50 per cent of the ideas in what she scanned. At the same time, it was felt that training in test preparation and test taking would be helpful to her. Eleanor's mother wondered aloud why Eleanor had not been taught how to take notes in high school. She said that she had been glancing through one of Eleanor's notebooks, noted the lack of organization of her class notes, and said as far as she could determine, Eleanor had never been taught that there was any value in taking notes on her reading assignments, since the girl never took notes while doing her homework. Eleanor's mother was assured that this aspect of study skills would not be overlooked.

Conference with Student

Eleanor was eager to begin her work at the clinic. She felt that she worked too slowly and was anxious to overcome this handicap as quickly as possible. She asked what the training would consist of and was told that the first step would be to provide a rapid phonic review to fill in the gaps in her understanding of phonic principles, with a view to giving her a conscious word attack. It was also mentioned that an analysis of words in terms of their phonic structure would facilitate her learning to spell difficult and unfamiliar words. Visual training would be embarked on immediately in order to create a greater capacity for reading and scanning rapidly. Her left-to-right eye-movement habits would be strengthened and her ability to move her eyes vertically, while seeking key words and phrases, would be developed. Eleanor said she felt that this was the training she needed.

Instruction Provided

In the initial phase of Eleanor's training, exercises in phonics and verbal structure were quickly covered until she gained conscious familiarity with the basic principles involved.

The level of her visual performance was high and tachistoscopic work produced rapid results. Her ability to perceive phrases of up to twenty-eight letters at flashes of one-one hundredth of a second was soon established, and she was reading in excess of five hundred words a minute on the eye-movement accelerator after only eight hours of training. At this point, the eye-masking element of the eye-movement device was eliminated since it was observed that Eleanor's left-to-right progression habits were firm and effective. She now read on the projection-accelerator device a full line at a time. Close observance of her reading with this device indicated that she was perceiving a line of print with only two or three fixations. Her comprehension scores of the material read on the device were at first about 50 per cent. It was explained to her that as her mind adjusted to the new reading speeds, comprehension would improve. By the time she had completed sixteen hours of work, Eleanor's comprehension scores on material read at speeds in excess of seven hundred words a minute were between 80 per cent and 100 per cent. At the same time, Eleanor was being given exercises on an individual pacing device. By the time she was reading above six hundred words per minute on the projection machine, her capacity for reading paced material began to increase. She was able to set the pacing device at nine hundred words per minute, at which speed she read with excellent comprehension. The activities on the individual pacer were supplemented with normal reading exercises which were closely timed. On some selections she found herself reading at speeds in excess of one thousand words per minute, with good comprehension. On more difficult material, she still found that she could retain most of the information contained in a selection at above six hundred words a minute.

It was decided that Eleanor's basic reading skills were now strong enough to enable her to develop efficient scanning and prereading habits. Study-skill training was also initiated. She was taught to preread a selection by surveying it to absorb as

193

much information as possible about it. She was taught to read the initial paragraph in order to determine the subject of the selection, to read the final paragraph in order to identify the writer's conclusions, and to read the key sentence of the intervening paragraphs in order to acquaint herself with the way in which the writer developed his ideas. She was also instructed to gather any information contained in headings, graphs, pictures, or captions before starting to read. She mastered these skills quickly.

Scanning presented a more difficult problem for Eleanor. Here she was expected to note key words and phrases as she swept her eyes down a column of print. She said that when she attempted to do this, she found herself left with an incoherent collection of information. In order to help her establish this skill, she was asked first to read the comprehension questions which followed each reading selection. Then on the individual pacing device, she was told to set the machine at a speed of twenty-five hundred words per minute. After scanning the selection at this controlled speed, she was to attempt to answer the questions. Having seen the question material before scanning, she was alerted to the important elements: those which should be sought out while scanning. After extensive practice with this technique, Eleanor was asked to scan the material without first going over the questions. She was happily surprised to find, after a time, that her comprehension scores after she had scanned material at speeds of close to three thousand words per minute were between 50 per cent and 70 per cent. She was now told that she should scan a selection at a speed in excess of three thousand words a minute to identify its general significance, then go back and read it at a speed of one thousand words per minute. She found that her comprehension scores following this procedure were usually 80 per cent to 100 per cent. Eleanor was becoming a proficient reader.

When Eleanor had learned to scan material effectively, she

was taught to take notes as she scanned. Note taking, it was pointed out to her, was easiest and the notes most valuable only after a thorough familiarity with the material under consideration had been achieved. Note taking was, therefore, best done after a selection had been preread, read, and while it was being gone over for a third time through the scanning process. The notes taken at this stage would contain only the main line of the writer's thoughts and would contain few irrelevancies. Details would not be mistaken for major ideas, as was so often the case when a student attempted to take notes during the first reading of a selection. It was pointed out to Eleanor that in studying complex material in this way, she would be encountering the material three times, each time aiming to organize the major ideas expressed. She would, therefore, have a far better chance of retaining the factual details and the underlying thinking of the writer than she could through a single reading.

Eleanor was now ready to learn the most effective means of preparing for an essay examination. Obviously, she was told, attempting to reread the assignments of a course before the examination was inefficient and could scarcely be expected to produce results. Even though a student might have good notes on both lecture and reading material, simply reading these notes over again would not provide the firm retention of material required.

It was necessary, she was told, to organize all of the material of the course into a coherent form. On an essay examination, a student was generally asked to identify a number of salient details, points which were probably emphasized in class as well as in the reading assignments, but the student would also be expected to provide a synthesis in essay form of the major concepts presented in a course.

Eleanor was told that most teachers prepare their courses methodically. The course material is organized by them carefully, so that an overall pattern of ideas will emerge. It is up

195

to the student to discern this pattern and to prepare for examinations by arranging the elements contained in such a pattern into a logical order. One of the easiest ways to do this would be to write a number of general questions which will anticipate the questions to be asked on the examination. These questions should cover all the aspects of the course treated up to the time of the examination. Then, through reference to both class and reading notes, these questions, which are in effect a master outline, should be answered in detail. The ideas and works studied and the concepts explored should all find a place within the framework established by the master outline.

Eleanor was assured that the very act of organizing the material would help set it in her mind. She was told that after the detailed outline had been completed, it should then be boiled down to a briefer outline composed of phrases or words which would immediately recall to her mind the more complete record of the course contained in her detailed outline. If she then memorized the boiled-down outline, she would waste no time when entering the examination room and would be ready to start writing at once. If this organizing of course material had been done well, Eleanor was told, she would find that the questions on the examination would differ only in emphasis from the ones she had expected. By following these steps, Eleanor could avoid spending valuable examination time in organizing her thoughts to conform to the questions encountered.

Eleanor said that a great number of examinations which she had taken and would have to take in the future were objective tests (multiple-choice or fill-in-the-blank-space tests), and she wanted to know the best way of preparing for them. She was told that since an objective test was concerned mainly with detailed factual information, she could best remember the details by studying in much the same way as for an essay test; elusive facts are elusive primarily because they are not easily related to other facts. Organizing course material means relating the separate elements of a course to each other. Having organized these elements into a pattern enables students to remember them.

But, Eleanor was told, there are a number of memory tricks that she could use to help her recall key information. One such memory device might be particularly useful in preparing for an objective test. She was told that most courses require that a student familiarize himself with a number of special terms. If these terms could be so arranged that their initial letters spelled a word, recall would be made easier. The aim of such a trick was to insure for the student in the examination room a rapid recall of all major areas of the subject that he was likely to be questioned on. The instructor said, "The student who leaves an examination room sick with the realization that he has forgotten an entire portion of course material, has not been guilty of carelessness or negligence so much as faulty preparation." Eleanor grinned knowingly, and admitted that this sort of thing had happened to her.

She was told that knowing *how to prepare* for an examination was important, but knowing *how to take* an objective test gave a student an additional advantage. Any exam should be approached without undue stress by a student who is properly prepared. But inevitably, some questions will not strike a responsive note when the student first glances at them. This is particularly true of objective tests. An essay examination is primarily a test of a student's ability to organize his thoughts. When he writes the test essay, he is disclosing the depth of his knowledge about the subject. At the same time, he is using the examination to help him complete the learning process. In some subjects, the essay examination tests the student's ability to express his ideas as much as his ability to retain and to organize them.

The objective examination, however, aims to inform the

197

teacher how well a student has grasped the information provided in a course. Eleanor said that she did not think objective examinations were very valuable. She said, for instance, that after cramming for an objective exam, she could usually do well on it, but if she had to take the same exam two weeks later, most of the facts would have departed.

She was told that the greatest value of such an examination probably lay in the studying a student engaged in in order to prepare himself for it. She had to admit that there were subjects in which the retention of a mass of factual information was in itself valuable and necessary. The medical student has to learn the names, positions, and uses of the bones of the body, and only an objective test can assure him, as well as his instructor, that these facts have been mastered.

On an objective test, the student's job is to show what he knows for his own sake as well as that of his teacher. In order to do this effectively, he first has to be fair to himself by possessing sufficient reading skill to complete the test.

Eleanor said that as a comparatively slow reader, she always felt under extreme pressure while taking an objective test because of the fear that she would not finish in time. She was told that the slow reader was rarely able to do justice to any test. Either he failed to complete enough of the test to show what he knew, or he forced himself to work at a speed beyond his capacity and made needless errors.

Eleanor asked if there had ever been any attempt made to figure out what effect reading ability had on the ability to take a test. She was told that many such studies had been made and that in every case, improved reading skills had shown marked improvement in test-taking ability. But she was told that reading skills alone were not the only element to be considered in taking an objective examination. The test-wise student always made a better showing than the one who just plunged into a test situation, nervously attempting to answer each question in turn.

Eleanor was told that she herself seemed to be unwilling to move on to the next question until she had expended every effort on the one at hand. This was just not sensible. She asked if there was a recommended approach. She was told that first she should read as rapidly as possible one question after another, answering only those questions of which she was absolutely certain. Questions which seemed within her grasp but not immediately answerable without further thought, should be checked with a single check, and those questions which she knew would be difficult for her should be checked with a double check. When she had gone through the entire test, answering only the questions of which she was sure, she should then go back and work on the single-checked questions. Once she had done her best on these, she should spend the remaining time on the double-checked ones. In this way, Eleanor was told, she would be sure that she received credit for what she knew. She would also find that by reading all of the questions, she would probably be reminded of certain facts which would help her to answer other questions.

Eleanor said that when she was younger, she would get so nervous about an examination that she would often sit in the examination room with a blank mind, unable to attempt any of the questions. After she had been through enough exams, however, this acute fear had left her. She still found herself tense when faced with taking an exam. She was told that by developing an efficient examination-taking technique, she could expect to build enough confidence to overcome her fears.

The examination-taking techniques discussed with Eleanor were then practiced by her at the clinic. She was given a number of objective sections of various achievement tests and, with her expert reading skills, found herself able to whip through these tests rapidly and accurately.

Progress Achieved

Eleanor received a total of thirty hours of training. Some of her scores were far above the standards established for the terminal test, so that no accurate measurement of her performance was possible. She was now confident that she was fully prepared to handle the challenges she would encounter in college, and there was little doubt but that she would be able to make maximum use of her abilities.

PART **III**

Appendix

Establishing Reading Laboratories in Schools

Most of the schools in America are aware of the desirability of establishing remedial and developmental reading programs. There is, however, confusion among educators, especially at the high-school level, as to the most effective course to be followed in establishing such programs. Questions regarding the equipment to purchase, test materials to use, organization of the classroom, diagnostic program to be relied on, grouping of students, and the scope of such a program must be answered in specific terms by each school contemplating the introduction of special reading instruction into the curriculum. Many schools have courageously attempted to answer these questions by setting up piecemeal programs. In many cases, such attempts have suffered because teachers have too often lacked familiarity with the instruments and materials available. In other cases, these programs have been unsuccessful because of the confusion generally attendant on working with new techniques. But the larger number of programs which do not seem to be achieving their aims have been handicapped by the fact that the programs themselves are too limited both in terms of the training they provide and the number of hours of instruction offered each week. Since the development of reading skills depends upon the establishment of firm habits, it is essential that students receive sufficiently intensive instruction. To expect lasting habits to be established through less than three to five hours of concentrated training each week is to invite disappointment. The most effective program will meet for an hour a day, five days a week, and will last a minimum of eight weeks. When reading skills are gained within the framework of a consistent and regularly experienced training period, the skills gained are more likely to be retained.

Another factor which interferes with the efficacy of many reading programs is a disproportionate student-teacher ratio. When this ratio is between thirty and fifty students to a teacher, as is frequently the case, the teacher cannot provide individual attention, and the less capable students find themselves profiting very little from the instruction. Skill learning of any kind requires close supervision and guidance. Small classes in which individual attention is possible are a prerequisite to success. Most schools, by making imaginative use of currently available staff, can provide enough teachers to establish a ten-to-one ratio for a reading program. This aim can often be achieved through the participation of a school librarian, a part-time reading consultant, or someone whose school duties are primarily administrative. For that matter, capable part-time help can often be found outside the school faculty.

A reading laboratory can be most effective if a specific room within the school is reserved exclusively for this purpose. Such a room should be furnished, designed, and equipped in consultation with someone whose experience and knowledge in the field qualifies him for this work. A properly designed reading laboratory can go a long way toward insuring the desired results. Separate activity spaces within the laboratory, so placed as to assure a smooth traffic flow, can help cut down on distraction.

of the students. A sample floor plan of a reading laboratory appears on page 237 of this book. Properly planned arrangement of activity spaces, in accordance with the instruments to be used in them, can help maintain a high level of interest on the part of students. Since any reading laboratory must provide training which is vital and active, materials used in such a laboratory must be readily accessible to both students and teachers and catalogued in accordance with a simple system which will allow the students themselves to keep the materials in good order.

The activities which can be successfully performed in a reading-laboratory situation include all those normally carried on in a regular classroom plus those requiring special equipment. Some of these activities are listed below:

To Develop Visual Perception

1. Group tachistoscopic exercises using *nonverbal* film-strip material
2. Group tachistoscopic exercises using *verbal* film-strip material
3. Individual tachistoscopic exercises using verbal and nonverbal material

To Develop Word Recognition Proficiency

Blackboard and workbook exercises as well as game-type and writing activities on:
1. Configuration or word-form clues
2. Picture and contextual clues
3. Structural analysis or word structure
   a. Compound words
   b. Roots, prefixes, and suffixes
   c. Contracted words
   d. Abbreviated words
   e. Syllabication

4. Phonics or phonetic analysis
   a. Vowels
   b. Consonants
   c. Diphthongs
   d. Digraphs
   e. Blends
   f. Silent letters
   g. Accent
   h. Consonant controllers of vowel sounds
5. Dictionary
   a. Phonetic keys
   b. Phonetic respelling

To Develop Meaning or Understanding

Oral and written exercises accompanied by oral discussion and explanation, and amplification based on questions inquiring into the following kinds of meanings:

1. Literal comprehension
   a. Understanding specific word meanings
   b. Identifying clearly stated facts and details
   c. Identifying various kinds of sequence
   d. Understanding punctuation
   e. Identifying referents
   f. Understanding double negatives
   g. Understanding unusual word order
   h. Understanding sentence structure
2. Interpretation
   a. Identifying implications
   b. Identifying assumptions
   c. Drawing conclusions
   d. Making generalizations
   e. Anticipating events and predicting outcomes
   f. Making comparisons and contrasts
   g. Perceiving relationships of various kinds
   h. Identifying character traits and motives
   i. Determining main idea

3. Critical Analysis or Evaluation
   a. Discriminating fact and opinion
   b. Recognizing ambiguities and discrepancies
   c. Identifying author's purpose, mood, tone, or intent
   d. Recognizing propaganda, slant, bias, prejudice
   e. Judging accuracy, relevancy, validity, value, authenticity, recency, completeness
   f. Identifying techniques author uses to accomplish his purpose
   g. Evaluating type and quality of writing
   h. Recognizing irony and sarcasm

To Develop Fluency and Speed

1. Normal timed-reading with elapsed time indicator
2. Individual reading-pacer exercises—reading function
3. Group eye-movement-control-acceleration projection device with film-strip materials—reading function
4. Group eye-movement-control-acceleration projection device with film-strip materials—scanning function
5. Individual reading-pacer exercises—scanning function

To Develop Study Skills

Exercises to give practice in:
1. Prereading, surveying, or overviewing
2. Skimming and scanning
3. Taking notes
4. Outlining
5. Reviewing
6. Preparing for and taking tests
7. Writing précis and compositions
8. Preparing and delivering reports and talks
9. Using resource materials
10. Research techniques

The day's class plans for any reading laboratory can be constructed from this checklist. Emphasis in instruction will, of course, depend upon the judgment of individual teachers as dictated by the problems of their students.

Diagnostic Program

A necessary part of each reading laboratory's function is the accurate diagnosis of reading difficulties. All students in a school should be given nationally standardized silent reading tests at regularly scheduled intervals. The results obtained on the reading tests should, of course, be checked against the results of intelligence, aptitude and other achievement tests, which should also be administered. The administrator of a school's reading program can gain a picture of a student's capacities and limitations from such test information, and a realistic program can be planned and provided for most students on the basis of these test results. Problem readers, however, need more extensive testing. More detailed information concerning their deficiencies may be obtained from diagnostic tests.

A diagnostic reading test is concerned specifically with the degree of reading skill possessed by any student in specific areas of reading. It is a performance test rather than an aptitude test, and an analysis of a diagnostic reading test requires that the person making the analysis keep in mind the fact that reading skill depends primarily upon two factors. In the first place, what is the student's level of verbal dexterity? In other words, how well can he be expected to learn to read? In the second place, does the student have the mechanical skills necessary for effective reading? Is visual perception well established, and does he have the ability to retain visual images accurately? In which reading skills is he deficient? Good diagnostic testing will provide answers to these questions.

Some tests which are useful for measuring reading achievement and identifying weaknesses in reading skills include the following:

Reading Achievement Tests

CALIFORNIA READING TESTS, 1957 Edition
 Lower Primary: Grades 1 and 2
 Primary: Grades 3 and 4
 Elementary: Grades 4-6
 Junior High: Grades 7-9
 Advanced: Grades 9-14
 Forms: AA, BB, CC, DD
 Published by California Test Bureau

COOPERATIVE ENGLISH TESTS, Test C: Reading Comprehension
 Test C1: Grades 7-12
 Test C2: College
 Forms: R, T, Y, Z
 Published by Educational Testing Service

IOWA SILENT READING TESTS, New Edition
 Elementary Test: Grades 4-8
 Advanced Test: Grades 9-13
 Forms: Am, Bm, Cm, Dm
 Published by Harcourt, Brace & World, Inc.

METROPOLITAN ACHIEVEMENT TESTS, Revised (1959)
 Primary I Battery: Grade 1
 Primary II Battery: Grades 2 and 3
 Elementary Reading: Grades 3 and 4
 Intermediate Reading: Grades 5 and 6
 Advanced Reading: Grades 7 and 8
 Forms: A and B
 Published by Harcourt, Brace & World, Inc.

SEQUENTIAL TEST OF EDUCATIONAL PROGRESS
 Level 4: Grades 4-6
 Level 3: Grades 7-9

Level 2: Grades 10-12
Level 1: College
Forms: A and B
Published by Educational Testing Service

SRA ACHIEVEMENT SERIES: READING
Grades 1 and 2
Grades 2-4
Grades 4-6
Grades 6-9
Forms: A and B
Science Research Associates, Inc.

STANFORD ACHIEVEMENT TESTS
Primary: Grades 1-3
Elementary: Grades 3 and 4
Intermediate: Grades 5 and 6
Advanced: Grades 7-9
Forms: J, K, L, M
Published by Harcourt, Brace & World, Inc.

Diagnostic Reading Tests

The tests in this group are generally useful at any grade level when pupils are experiencing difficulty in the basic skills of reading.

BOTEL READING INVENTORY
Only one form and level
Published by Follett Publishing Company

DIAGNOSTIC READING TESTS
Kindergarten through Grade 4
Lower Level: Grades 4-6
Higher Level: Grades 7-13
Forms: A and B
Published by Committee on Diagnostic Tests

DOREN DIAGNOSTIC READING TEST
Only one form and level
Published by American Guidance Service, Inc.

DURRELL ANALYSIS OF READING DIFFICULTY
Only one form and level
Published by Harcourt, Brace & World, Inc.

GATES READING DIAGNOSTIC TESTS, Revised
Only one form and level
Published by Bureau of Publications, Teachers College, Columbia University

ROSWELL-CHALL DIAGNOSTIC READING TEST
Only one form and level
Published by Essay Press

SILENT READING DIAGNOSTIC TESTS
Only one form and level
Published by Lyons and Carnahan

In addition to administering tests, much valuable diagnostic information may be obtained from observing pupils as they work on any reading tests and exercises as well as from informal inventories and checklists based on assignments in readers and textbooks.

Possible Inhibiting Factors

Each student who is experiencing severe reading difficulty should be carefully observed for evidence of poor physical co-ordination which may be interfering with the development of academic skills. Where any serious deficiency is suspected, consultation with a school psychologist should take place before instruction is initiated.

The identification of any physical obstacles to reading development should be considered one of the most important purposes of a diagnostic program. Each student's vision and hearing should be screened to eliminate deficiencies in these areas as causes for impediments to learning. Since one of the commonly encountered physiological obstacles to the development of reading skills is mixed-lateral dominance, a dominance test should be administered to all severely retarded students before they start any remedial program. Some of the screening tests and instruments which are available for these purposes include the following:

Visual Screening Tests

AMERICAN OPTICAL SCHOOL
VISION SCREENING TEST
American Optical Company
Buffalo 15, New York

KEYSTONE VISUAL SURVEY TESTS
Keystone View Company
Meadville, Pennsylvania

ORTHO-RATER
Bausch and Lomb, Inc.
Rochester 2, New York

T/O SCHOOL VISION TESTER
Titmus Optical Company, Inc.
Petersburg, Virginia

Auditory Screening Tests

AUDIOMETER
Maico Company, Inc.
Minneapolis, Minnesota

AUDIOMETER
Western Electric Company
New York, New York

Tests of Lateral Dominance

HARRIS TESTS OF LATERAL DOMINANCE, Revised
The Psychological Corporation
304 East 45th Street
New York 17, New York

THE KEYSTONE TESTS OF BINOCULAR SKILL
  Keystone View Company
  Meadville, Pennsylvania

SPACHE BINOCULAR READING TEST
  Keystone View Company
  Meadville, Pennsylvania

Selection of Devices and Materials

Tachistoscopic Training

Effective reading requires effective visual habits. Since we read a line of print through a series of fixations, our eyes stopping to take in a visual image, moving to take in another, and so forth, in an arbitrary left-to-right direction, it is essential that efficient visual-perception habits be established.

Each fixation must, in itself, make it possible for the reader to perceive a maximum amount of material. In other words, the eye span must be extended, so that the student is able to see groups of words instead of single words. A wide span of recognition is a concomitant of good reading.

Achieving a broader visual "grasp" or "bite" must be accompanied by more rapid seeing. The lapse of time that occurs between the instant that the eyes perceive an image and the moment that the reader reacts to it must be cut to a minimum. When starting training, many slow readers will take from one to one-and-a-half seconds between the time a visual target is flashed on a screen and the time they start to write what they have seen. This time lapse can be cut dramatically.

The tachistoscope is a device which for years has been found most useful in developing visual perception. Tachistoscopic devices designed for group use are instruments which project a visual target on a screen. The target is contained on either film strips or glass slides. The operator of the machine changes the targets and causes them to flash on the screen at speeds of anywhere from two seconds to one one-hundredth of a second, depending upon the complexity of the image flashed and the skill of the students. The operator alerts the class to the fact that an image is to be flashed. He then flashes the image. The students write what they are able to perceive of the image. The operator then brings the image back to the screen for examination and comparison, and in the case of phonic exercises, for discussion of phonic structure. The cycle is then repeated with another target image. In considering the selection of a tachistoscopic device, the physiological effect of the operation of the device must be taken into account. To flash a bright light on a screen in a semidarkened room causes retinal shock. It should be remembered that in a room which has a low level of light, the pupil of the eye is distended. Flashing a bright light momentarily makes the pupil contract. Immediately, however, the room is again dimly lit, and the pupil distends. Prolonged exercises, even drills lasting five minutes, tend to produce eye strain under these conditions. No particular damage to the eyes has been noted, but the effect of such activity is the comparatively rapid production of eye fatigue, a condition which naturally cuts down the length of a training session and the value of the training itself. Another factor to be considered is that a negative retinal after-image is produced for many people when a bright image is flashed in a darkened room. Some students, it has been reported, become adept at reading this after-image, and the effectiveness of the training is thereby diminished. A device which can provide a constant level of light on the screen and can be used in a normally lit classroom, is, therefore, desirable.

The limits of usefulness of the tachistoscope have scarcely been tapped. Naturally, the effectiveness of the device for teach-

215

ing purposes is determined largely by the program material used with each machine. Visual exercises consisting of non-verbal target materials have been designed to develop visual proficiency in terms both of horizontal and vertical seeing tasks. Targets consisting of numbers, of mixed letters, of abstract symbols, of drawings, etc., all have their respective place in any program.

There is no doubt but that training with this device increases visual capacity and accuracy. The target images, when flashed at a speed faster than one-tenth of a second, must be perceived with one eye fixation. Perception, in this regard, means noting and holding in the mind an accurate representation of the flashed image. Co-ordinational skills are called into play. The mind must react quickly and accurately to the impulses presented it by the eyes. The flashed images must be retained and, inasmuch as lack of visual retention is one of the problems frequently facing the beginning reader, the development of this skill is essential to satisfactory progress.

It is therefore suggested that visual training with nonverbal materials, with pictures of familiar objects such as cats, dogs, ducks, and geese, be provided at the reading-readiness stage. In kindergarten, many teachers provide training in auditory discrimination, but comparatively little is done with the development of visual discrimination.

It might be mentioned at this point that the student who has difficulty in establishing directional habits which are necessary to reading and writing can be helped through tachistoscopic work also. Whether the student's difficulty stems from mixed-lateral dominance or from the fact that five- and six-year-olds inevitably tend to reverse symbols, since the directional pattern necessary to reading and writing skills has not yet been established, emphasis should be directed, as early as possible, to the development of consistent left-to-right progressional habits. At a more advanced level, the student must note such subtle things as the "a" preceding the "i" in spelling the word "afraid." At kindergarten level, he should practice observing that in a picture showing a row of animals, the cat comes before the dog or the horse comes before the cow; "before" in this case meaning "to the left of." By doing so, he will be ready for the more subtle discriminations at more advanced levels.

At advanced levels, when working with students who are reasonably good readers and spellers, the emphasis of training needs to be shifted to the development of a high order of visual skills and the retention of increasingly complex visual targets. Phrase materials are helpful in this regard. Again, directional factors must be considered of paramount importance. For one thing, the student must be taught to focus on the left margin of the image to be flashed. The student who focuses on the center of the image will generally find that he sees the material to the right of his focal point. Inasmuch as we read English from left to right, our eye span has been automatically trained to loop out to the right, and we unconsciously tend to suppress material which appears to the left of our focal point. If a three-word phrase is flashed, it is better that the student see the first word than that he see the second and third words but not the first. The habit of perceiving a verbal image from the left must be established in order further to strengthen left-to-right directional patterns of reading. The student who develops a habit of focusing on the center of a word is in danger of developing habits of regression.

"Near-Point" Tachistoscopic Training

The use of the group tachistoscope is necessary with primary-grade children for several reasons, not the least of which is the fact that it capitalizes on their natural farsightedness. With more advanced students, individual tachistoscopic devices can prove effective. These "near-point" tachistoscopes provide the teacher with the opportunity for greater flexibility in programming. They are also valuable since, as is true with any individually operated instrument, the student is enabled to work at his own pace. The selection of a "near-point" tachistoscope should be based on its adaptability to the entire reading program. The availability of target materials is, of course, an important factor. For a laboratory program, it is desirable that the same targets used for group tachistoscopic exercises be available for "near-point" tachistoscopic work and these target materials should, of course, be correlated in terms of verbal exercises with the reading exercises that are also a part of any laboratory program.

Among the tachistoscopes that are available at the present time are the following:

Distance-Projection Tachistoscopes

AVR EYE-SPAN TRAINER
Audio-Visual Research Company
531 South Plymouth Court
Chicago 5, Illinois

COMPLETELY AUTOMATIC PROJECTION TACHISTO-SCOPE
Lafayette Instruments Company
North 26th and 52nd By-Pass
Lafayette, Indiana

CONSTANT ILLUMINATION TACHISTOSCOPE
Lafayette Instruments Company
North 26th and 52nd By-Pass
Lafayette, Indiana

KEYSTONE TACHISTOSCOPE
Keystone View Company
Meadville, Pennsylvania

218

TACH-X
Educational Developmental Laboratories
284 Pulaski Road
Huntington, New York

TACHIST-O-TIMER
Learning Through Seeing
259 East Erie Street
Chicago 11, Illinois

Near-Point Tachistoscopes

FLASH-X
Educational Developmental Laboratories
284 Pulaski Road
Huntington, New York

KEYSTONE TACHETTE
Keystone View Company
Meadville, Pennsylvania

TACHITRON
Lafayette Instruments Company
North 26th and 52nd By-Pass
Lafayette, Indiana

Eye-Movement Control Training

The most recent order of devices to gain popularity in the reading-training field are the eye-movement control machines. These devices perform a valuable function. They aim at establishing smooth left-to-right eye-movement control by forcing students to read without regressing or loitering. For example, part of a reading selection is projected on the screen, but only an area wide enough to reveal a few words at a time is left unmasked. The open area moves from left to right across a line. When it has completed its sweep, the next line of print is revealed and the moving window again sweeps from left to right. The student's eyes must follow the window.

219

The value of the eye-movement accelerators lies primarily in the fact that eye-movement training is provided at the same time as habits of acceleration are being developed. These machines are useful at the primary levels in helping to establish directional habits, and at the advanced levels marked increases in reading speed may be achieved. The co-ordinational aspects of reading skill are heightened through the use of these devices. The visual capacities gained through tachistoscopic training are here put to work. It is unfortunate that many schools which have purchased eye-movement accelerators have neglected to purchase any tachistoscopic devices, since basic visual training can best be accomplished with the tachistoscope. Where a choice between the purchase of a tachistoscope or an eye-movement accelerator faces a school district, it is recommended that the tachistoscope be chosen. The two devices together complement each other, but where only one can be bought, the tachistoscope is the more valuable.

A great deal of confusion has recently been created through claims that some students are taught to read at speeds of five, ten, and even twenty thousand words per minute. More accurately, this performance should be described as scanning, and extremely effective scanning performance can be gained. However, it should be pointed out that before such efficient scanning techniques can be achieved, a student must develop efficient eye movement and co-ordinational skills. His normal reading of narrative material should be done easily at five hundred to seven hundred words per minute with excellent understanding. Only when he is able to read in this fashion can he expect to develop really effective scanning skills.

Some examples of these devices are the following:

Eye-Movement Control Devices

CONTROLLED READER SERIES
Educational Developmental Laboratories

284 Pulaski Road
Huntington, New York

CRAIG READER
Craig Research Inc.
3410 South La Cienega Blvd.
Los Angeles 16, California

PHRASE READING
C-B Educational Films, Inc.
703 Market Street
San Francisco 4, California

SKIMMER
Educational Developmental Laboratories
284 Pulaski Road
Huntington, New York

Individual Pacing Devices

These devices are probably more numerous than any others. Their principle is very simple. A shutter bar descends from the top to the bottom of a page at a controlled rate. The student's reading speed must be such that he stays ahead of the moving shutter. He is, in effect, racing against the occluding shutter bar.

No one pacing device has any particular advantage over any other one now available. They all perform the same function in approximately the same way, with the exception of a machine which uses, instead of an opaque bar as a shutter, a shadow. The advantage of this innovation is questionable. The major concern of anyone who is contemplating the purchase of such devices for use within schools would seem to be the sturdiness of the device and, naturally, its cost. Reading pacers are used individually by each student. They receive rough handling, and any fragile elements give way rapidly. Some of these

221

devices make noise, which is distracting, and the more silent the machine, the more desirable. Some of these devices are operated electrically. Those which require plugging into a wall outlet are naturally less flexible, since they cannot be carried and used in any location not close to a wall outlet. Others are battery operated and have the obvious disadvantage inherent in such a device. An instrument which is compact, non-electric, extremely sturdy, and completely silent is, therefore, the most desirable.

The reading pacer has limited usefulness for the primary grades. Its purpose is to increase reading speed. It is fruitless to be concerned about speed as such in the first and second grades. By the third grade, some concern should be felt for students who are working very slowly but who have no word-recognition problems, since extreme slowness indicates a lack of fluency, and lack of fluency interferes with comprehension. Lack of fluency at this stage very often attests to the fact that the student has not developed a sufficiently large sight vocabulary and is not in possession of effective word-recognition skills. But also important is the fact that such halting readers may not have established smooth eye-movement habits. The pacer does not assist the student in acquiring eye-movement skills and should not be used until such skills are in the student's possession. At the primary level, an eye-movement accelerator is more helpful.

The reading pacer, therefore, is best introduced into any reading program at fourth-grade level or above. It should be used at first with very simple material. Since establishing habits of speed interferes initially with a student's understanding of what he is reading, it is wise to introduce him to more rapid reading speeds with material which is easily comprehended; otherwise, there is danger that the student will lose the habit of seeking meaning in what he reads. He may begin to feel that

222

the important thing is simply to get through the material without understanding it. The most effective way, in general, of insuring that a student does not lose a feeling of responsibility for understanding whatever he reads, whether on one of the devices or in normal reading, is to have him questioned on whatever material he covers. This is particularly true when an acceleration device of any sort is being employed, since the tendency to keep up with the device's pace, regardless of comprehension, may become the student's primary aim.

The reading pacer should be regarded merely as a developmental tool. There is a tendency to regard it as a cure-all. Lavishly advertised programs aimed at adult readers seem to assure them that through use of this device, all of their reading problems will be overcome. It must be emphasized that this device, as is true with any others, is valuable only to the degree that it is incorporated into and used intelligently in a comprehensive reading program.

Perhaps the greatest advantage of the reading pacer is its value in helping students retain habits of rapid reading that have been gained through a thorough program of training. A reader who has developed his skills to a high level should read with a pacer a few times a week to make sure that the skills become well habituated, or he may slip back into his former laboriously slow habits.

The pacer can be a valuable aid in the development of scanning techniques. By setting the device at speeds of fifteen hundred to three thousand words a minute and attempting to identify key words and phrases at this rate, a student will find that he is forced to scan. He simply cannot keep ahead of the rapidly descending bar at these speeds otherwise.

Students find use of pacers particularly helpful as they progress to higher grade levels and encounter more complex terms and concepts. The challenge imposed as they move to higher grades has a tendency to slow them down, and they can easily revert to inefficient reading habits. A reading pacer provides some insurance against this eventuality.

Among the popularly used pacers that are available are the following:

Reading Pacers

AVR RATEOMETER
Audio-Visual Research Company
531 South Plymouth Court
Chicago 5, Illinois

KEYSTONE READING PACER
Keystone View Company
Meadville, Pennsylvania

READING RATE CONTROLLER
Stereo-Optical Company
3539 North Kenton Avenue
Chicago 41, Illinois

SHADOWSCOPE READING PACER
Lafayette Instruments Company
North 26th and 52nd By-Pass
Lafayette, Indiana

SRA READING ACCELERATOR
Science Research Associates
259 East Erie Street
Chicago 11, Illinois

Materials for an Automated Reading Program

Careful selection of reading materials is an important factor in setting up a reading laboratory. Reading materials should include books of reading selections; comprehension question materials which emphasize the development of both interpretive skills and retention of factual information; vocabulary exercises keyed to the requirements of the reading materials; film-strip materials, also appropriately keyed; diagnostic and achievement reading tests; and phonic workbooks for primary levels.

There is available a variety of reading materials at all grade levels. Graded reading material for school use has usually been edited in accordance with the formulas for reading difficulty established by such measures as the Thorndike-Lorge, Dale-Chall, or the Flesch readability formulas. These formulas take into account such factors as vocabulary difficulty, length of sentences, personal as opposed to abstract qualities, etc. Slavish concern with such formulas can lead to material so watered down that interest level may be diluted almost to the vanishing point, but they have obvious usefulness as guides to difficulty.

Since a sight system of reading requires that the student be exposed to certain words again and again in order to achieve recognition of them, the writer of primary material finds himself so limited by the vocabulary he can use that it is almost impossible for him to write anything that is very exciting. The writer who is preparing material for students who are achieving at higher levels and who are skillful in phonics is in a better situation. It is necessary that students who are learning to read through a phonic system encounter in their reading numerous words which are unfamiliar in written form. These words should not, of course, be outside their speaking or hearing vocabulary. But it is essential that students who are building word-attack skills have the opportunity to exercise these skills on words that are new to them.

An effectively programmed reading course provides the opportunity for students to encounter the same words numerous times in different contexts. Preferably, these words should be susceptible to phonic interpretation initially but, too, the student must be given the chance to build his sight vocabulary.

Prior to reading any given selection, the student should work with the more difficult words to be encountered in that selection. These words should be previewed on the blackboard, and the phonic instruction for that day should be drawn from these particular words. Syllabication of words, preceded by the identification of any common prefixes or suffixes and compound words, should be done first. The initial consonant sounds should be identified and then the vowel sounds determined. When the words have been identified, a discussion of the meaning of these words should then take place, and at appropriate levels (from third or fourth grade, depending upon the reading skill of the particular group), dictionary work should be introduced. Students should write sentences containing key words to gain further familiarity with them.

When a student is reading under normal conditions, without devices, an elapsed-time indicator, or large clock with a sweep secondhand, is particularly helpful. It should be mounted on the front wall of the room, and students should be taught how to time their own work. From third-grade level, it is important for students to be conscious of the fact that they must read with reasonable speed. Reading selections, starting at this grade level, should contain word-count information which will enable the student to figure out his word-per-minute rate. Habits of fluency can be achieved most readily when reading is related to the time factor. It will generally be found that the first few times students read under timed conditions, they tend to rush beyond their capacity, with the result that they understand little of what they read. An antidote to this practice is found in the comprehension questions which must accompany each reading selection. Reading without understanding is pointless.

NOTE: Specific information with regard to instruments and correlated teaching materials available for use in a reading laboratory can be found in catalogues of individual manufacturers and publishers. The National Audio-Visual Association publishes an annual catalogue which contains information on many of the devices now available. Local audio-visual dealers should be consulted as should the appropriate departments of the National Education Association and State Teachers' Associations. In the final analysis, however, the help of an experienced and qualified reading consultant, who is able to work closely with a school district, should be obtained.

Specific books and workbooks useful for teaching reading skills will not be listed here, since they are far too numerous. Instead, the reader is directed to consult sources such as *Good Reading for Poor Readers* by George D. Spache (Champaign, Illinois: Garrard Publishing Co., 1962) for suggestions. *Good Reading for Poor Readers* contains annotated lists of trade books, adapted classics, textbooks, workbooks, games, magazines, newspapers, series books, book clubs, and indexes of reading lists. Reading levels as well as interest levels are indicated for about a thousand items useful with retarded readers.

Grouping of Students, Class Plans, and Physical Arrangement of Laboratory

All classes should be divided into three groups or more. The aim is to achieve a homogeneity of reading skills within each group. Any teacher can easily see that with the laboratory activities listed above, each group can be kept fruitfully employed in a different activity simultaneously. The teacher's presence is most necessary for those groups engaged in receiving phonic instruction and group tachistoscopic exercises. After initial familiarization, students can perform a large measure of all other exercises with only partial supervision.

The emphasis at this level should be on the establishment of a firm knowledge of phonic and verbal structure. Exercises on the blackboard should be so planned that the students themselves write on the blackboard. This enables the teacher to evaluate accurately their grasp of the instruction. Also, this approach changes a passive lesson into a stimulating one, since the students participate actively.

Auditory discrimination usually needs to be emphasized at this level. The students must learn to hear the sounds of the letters within the words they write. Verbal tachistoscopic exercises which are keyed to the vocabulary demands of reading selections to be used in the same period provide the words which can be drawn on for the particular phonic instruction of that day.

During any class session, each of the groups should engage in at least three activities to prevent boredom and fatigue. Through proper arrangement of the laboratory, after each activity has been completed within a predetermined time period, the groups should rotate. The physical movement after each period helps to sustain a high level of interest, as does the variety of activities provided.

During any one period, the teacher should aim at providing work on either the group or individual tachistoscope, on the blackboard, and on some type of reading exercise followed immediately by comprehension and vocabulary activities. These three major activities should use correlated material. Thus, the verbal demands provided by the reading exercises should be regarded as the basis for both blackboard and tachistoscopic work.

As a general rule, devices should be used in direct ratio to the reading skill possessed by the students. It will be found that the primary remedial groups will gain little benefit from acceleration devices until fluency has been achieved. On the other hand, tachistoscopic training related directly to phonic analysis will be found particularly helpful in developing basic verbal skills. Nonverbal tachistoscopic work is valuable for all groups, since basic visual skills are gained in this way. The sessions of nonverbal visual training should be limited to five minutes at this level.

To facilitate explanation in the following discussion of the sort of class plans that might be set up for this level, the three groups will be identified in the following charts as A, B, and C groups. Group A is the slower group, Group B the average, and Group C the most advanced. Class sessions consist of fifty-minute periods.

For the first twenty minutes, the teacher will work with the B and C groups on the group tachistoscope, spending five minutes on nonverbal exercises and fifteen minutes on verbal exercises. The A group will do individual tachistoscopic work on less advanced material. All tachistoscopic work will cover vocabulary demands required for the reading exercises that follow. During the following ten-minute period, the B group will read on the eye-movement accelerator at a speed suitable for that group. The C group will read the same selection on the individual reading pacers. Meanwhile, the A group will read its easier material on the individual reading pacers also. When the three groups have completed their reading, they will spend an additional ten minutes answering questions. The final ten minutes can be spent by the A group on blackboard work, so that the teacher can cover phonic principles raised by the vocabulary demands of the selection they have just read. The B group, meanwhile, can work on enrichment activities, while the members of the C group time themselves on another reading selection, which is read normally without devices, though timed.

The following chart represents this class plan:

Minutes	20	10	10	10
A Group	Ind. Tach.	Ind. Pacer	Question	(T) Phonics
B Group	(T) Group Tach.	(T) Group Eye-Mvt. Accel.	Question	Enrich. Act.
C Group	(T) Group Tach.	Ind. Pacer	Question	Normal-Timed Reading

In order further to clarify the above class plan, the movement of each group within a conventional classroom is demonstrated below.

In the charts below, the three groups are designated by the letters A, B, and C. The (T) signifies where the presence of the teacher will be most valuable at that particular time.

First: 20-minute period	
Group Tach.* B (T) C	Group Accel.*
A Tach. Indiv.* Activity	Indiv.* Activity

Second: 10-minute period	
Group Tach.	Group Accel. B (T)
A Pacer Indiv. Activity	C Pacer Indiv. Activity

* These terms refer to activity areas, not necessarily to the activities themselves.

230

Third: 10-minute period		Fourth: 10-minute period	
Group Tach.	Group Accel. B ? Questions	Group Tach. A (T) Phonics	Group Accel.
A ? Questions Indiv. Act.	C ? Questions Indiv. Act.	C Normal Rdg. Indiv. Act.	B Enrich. Indiv. Act.

Since movement of the students from one part of the classroom to another for each activity is desirable, the movement of each group is plotted below:

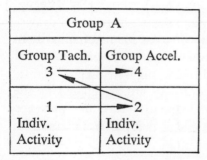

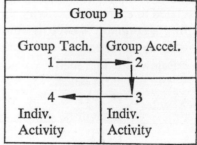

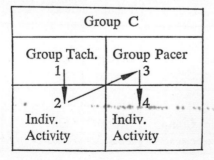

From the above diagrams, it should be possible to grasp the basic mechanics in setting up a laboratory program. The ingenuity of the teacher comes into play once familiarity has been established with the various activities made available. The value of a laboratory program to any school lies in the fact that through careful administration of the activities outlined here, each student is assured of receiving a maximum amount of individual help. The teacher is free to devote her time to those areas of instruction which demand her attention. The other aspects of reading, those which depend for the most part upon development of skill through practice, can be efficiently provided by the self-administered exercises on devices. For one thing, the use of mechanical aids increases student motivation to a marked degree. Drill exercises which are monotonous and lead to boredom and loss of interest seem to gain in interest when done with instruments. Since each activity is directly related to each other activity through the use of material drawn from a common source, a battery of coherent reading skills is being developed.

Below are included two additional suggested class plans:

Minutes:	15	10	10	15
Group A	(T) Phonics	Ind. Tach.	(T) Group Accel.	Questions
Group B	Ind. Tach.	Group Accel.	Questions	(T) Enrichment Activities
Group C	Ind. Comp. Exercises	(T) Group Tach.	Ind. Pacer	Questions

Minutes:	15	15	20
Group A	(T) Group Tach.	Group Accel.	Ind. Comp. Exercises
Group B	(T) Group Tach.	Ind. Pacer, Q.	(T) Enrich. Activities
Group C	Indiv. Tach.	(T) Blackboard Spelling	Normal Reading, Questions

Junior High School and High School, Developmental Programs

The aim in high-school developmental reading programs is to insure that every student achieve the maximum degree of skill of which he is capable. The aim of any laboratory program must be to give each student a versatility of reading abilities. He must have at his command a number of different reading and study skills, and he must be able to apply the appropriate skill to each academic problem that he faces. It would, for instance, be senseless for a student to read his chemistry text as he would read a newspaper or a novel.

The initial concern at this level should be that each student become a fluent and understanding reader. Any student who is not reading narrative material of average difficulty at three hundred words per minute is severely handicapped for a number of reasons. It will be very difficult for him to develop effective understanding skills and, equally important, he will be unable, since eye movement and co-ordination are poorly developed, to learn efficient prereading or scanning techniques.

233

Once the members of a developmental class are reading at a fluent rate, scanning activities should be introduced into the program. These activities can be performed on the individual reading pacer or on the group eye-movement control device or in normal reading exercises. Scanning activities can either precede the reading of a selection or, for purposes of establishing efficient note-taking skills, the scanning can be done after a selection has been read and before the question material has been attempted. In the former instance, the scanning becomes, in effect, a prereading exercise. This kind of prereading gives the student a means of identifying specific information in an unread selection. It is particularly valuable in helping a student engaged in research decide whether or not a given piece of reading contains information which is relevant to his purpose.

Below are set forth two suggested class plans which include study-skills training:

Minutes:	15	10	10	15
Group A	(T) Group Tach.	(T) Group Accel.	Questions	Individual Comprehension Exercises
Group B	Individual Tach.	Individual Pacer	Questions Test Instrument	(T) Enrich. Activities
Group C	Group Accel. Scanning Function	Read Questions without Answering	Individual Tach.	Group Accel. Answer Questions

Minutes:	15	10	10	15
Group A	Ind. Pacer Scan	Group Tach.	Group Accel. Read	Questions
Group B	Group Tach.	Group Accel.	Questions	Ind. Pacer Scan-Take Notes
Group C	Individual Tach.	Individual Pacer	Questions	Enrich. Activities

Although the class plans presented may appear confusing at first, it takes a class no more than two sessions to grasp the routine, and every variation in the program is thereafter greeted with an additional heightening of interest. The first law when working with children is, of course, that interest be maintained. If interest is lost, learning stops. Children are not bored by challenging and difficult material as much as they are by static and uninteresting teaching activities.

The programs discussed above rely on a balance of automated and conventional techniques. The use of instruments provides a teacher with effective tools which can help individualize teaching. On the other hand, even without the use of devices, the imaginative teacher can establish a variety of nonautomated teaching activities which will develop reading skill. By rotating groups of students from one of these activities to another, lethargy can be avoided and minds kept alert.

Timed reading exercises, individual comprehension exercises, word games on the blackboard, phonic instruction, study-skills techniques, enrichment activities, comprehension- and vocabulary-question exercises: none of these require any mechanized accessories, and they provide training in all essential areas of reading skills.

235

The devices, however, serve to strengthen motivation, to speed the pace of activities, and to provide controls that insure effective use of time.

As any teacher knows, children grow animated and interested when they are in the midst of even the simplest sort of change. Just moving desks and chairs into an unfamiliar grouping will in itself arouse a great deal of interest in a classroom. An imaginative teacher can find additional ways to vary the conventional classroom pattern in terms both of physical arrangement and teaching activities.

Conclusion

The establishment of reading laboratories in our schools can help solve the problems of poor reading and disorganized study habits which plague so many of our youngsters. The efficacy of any such laboratory depends upon the skill and knowledge underlying its operation as well as on the proper selection of devices and pedagogical materials. The work of any reading laboratory should be correlated with the demands made on students by subject departments, and the cooperation of subject teachers in the arrangement of teaching programs can and should be obtained.

It is, however, of utmost importance that any reading laboratory be established and administered by teachers with a broad and deep knowledge of the field of reading. Too many school reading laboratories have failed to achieve their goals because the task of operating them was left to people who possessed neither training nor interest in this kind of work.

Some reading problems will always exist, but too many problem readers are made—not born. Ways of imparting necessary reading and study skills to all students who have the capacity are available. These ways must be adopted and put into use.

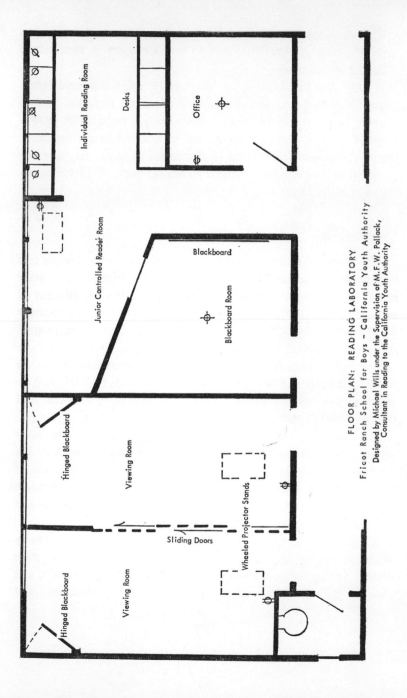

FLOOR PLAN: READING LABORATORY

Fricot Ranch School for Boys – California Youth Authority

Designed by Michael Wills under the Supervision of M.F.W. Pollack,
Consultant in Reading to the California Youth Authority

Index

241